Dreams of Lovers and Lies of Poets
Poetry, Knowledge, and Desire in the 'Roman de la Rose'

LEGENDA

LEGENDA, founded in 1995 by the European Humanities Research Centre of the University of Oxford, is now a joint imprint of the Modern Humanities Research Association and Maney Publishing. Titles range from medieval texts to contemporary cinema and form a widely comparative view of the modern humanities, including works on Arabic, Catalan, English, French, German, Greek, Italian, Portuguese, Russian, Spanish, and Yiddish literature. An Editorial Board of distinguished academic specialists works in collaboration with leading scholarly bodies such as the Society for French Studies and the British Comparative Literature Association.

MHRA

The Modern Humanities Research Association (MHRA) encourages and promotes advanced study and research in the field of the modern humanities, especially modern European languages and literature, including English, and also cinema. It also aims to break down the barriers between scholars working in different disciplines and to maintain the unity of humanistic scholarship in the face of increasing specialization. The Association fulfils this purpose primarily through the publication of journals, bibliographies, monographs and other aids to research.

Maney Publishing is one of the few remaining independent British academic publishers. Founded in 1900 the company has offices both in the UK, in Leeds and London, and in North America, in Boston. Since 1945 Maney Publishing has worked closely with learned societies, their editors, authors, and members, in publishing academic books and journals to the highest traditional standards of materials and production.

RESEARCH MONOGRAPHS IN FRENCH STUDIES

The *Research Monographs in French Studies* (RMFS) form a separate series within the Legenda programme and are published in association with the Society for French Studies. Individual members of the Society are entitled to purchase all RMFS titles at a discount.

The series seeks to publish the best new work in all areas of the literature, thought, theory, culture, film and language of the French-speaking world. Its distinctiveness lies in the relative brevity of its publications (50,000–60,000 words). As innovation is a priority of the series, volumes should predominantly consist of new material, although, subject to appropriate modification, previously published research may form up to one third of the whole. Proposals may include critical editions as well as critical studies. They should be sent with one or two sample chapters for consideration to Professor Ann Jefferson, New College, Oxford OX1 3BN.

PUBLISHED IN THIS SERIES

www.rmfs.mhra.org.uk

Dreams of Lovers and Lies of Poets

Poetry, Knowledge, and Desire in the Roman de la Rose

❖

SYLVIA HUOT

LEGENDA

Research Monographs in French Studies 31
Modern Humanities Research Association and Maney Publishing
2010

Published by the
Modern Humanities Research Association and Maney Publishing
1 Carlton House Terrace
London SW1Y 5AF
United Kingdom

LEGENDA is an imprint of the
Modern Humanities Research Association and Maney Publishing

Maney Publishing is the trading name of W. S. Maney & Son Ltd,
whose registered office is at Suite 1C, Joseph's Well, Hanover Walk, Leeds LS3 1AB

ISBN 978-1-906540-80-7

First published 2010

Printed in Great Britain

Cover: 875 Design

Copy-Editor: Richard Correll

CONTENTS

ACKNOWLEDGEMENTS

This study was carried out under the auspices of the project 'Poetic Knowledge in Late Medieval France', based at the Universities of Cambridge and Manchester, and funded by the Arts and Humanities Research Council. It has benefited greatly from discussions with the project participants: Adrian Armstrong and Rebecca Dixon of Manchester University, Sarah Kay of Princeton University and Finn Sinclair of Cambridge University. I am also grateful to Pembroke College, Cambridge for grants from the Fellows' Research Fund; and to both Pembroke College and the University of Cambridge for a sabbatical leave that allowed me to complete the first draft of the book.

My ideas in course of this project have been greatly enriched in ongoing conversations with my Cambridge colleagues Bill Burgwinkle, Miranda Griffin and Michael Reeve; my graduate student Beatrice Priest; Simon Gaunt of King's College, London; Karma Lochrie and Emanuel Mickel of Indiana University, Bloomington; and Jim Schultz of the University of California, Los Angeles. I am grateful to David Rollo of the University of Southern California for allowing me to read his as-yet unpublished study, 'A Brother to Hermaphroditus: Pleasure, Reference, and Sexuality in Medieval Narrative'. The opportunity to work with Stephen Nichols and Nadia Altschul, both of Johns Hopkins University, on the *Roman de la Rose* website project <http://romandelarose.org>, funded by the Andrew W. Mellon Foundation, has also been invaluable in keeping me constantly in contact with the *Rose* and its manuscripts, and with a host of questions concerning the reading and reception of the poem. My thoughts about the *Rose* and the Latin poets have been further nurtured and challenged over the years by family, friends, students and colleagues, both at home and around the world; this statement must suffice in expressing my thanks to all of them.

INTRODUCTION

The *Roman de la Rose*, self-styled 'art of love', freely acknowledges its own impossibility. Cupid, under whose auspices the poem is purportedly written, portrays the experience of erotic desire as something quintessentially impossible to express in literary form:[1]

> Li dex d'Amors lors me respont
> et ma demande bien m'espont. (*RR*, 2581–82)
>
> 'nes qu'em puet espuisier la mer,
> ne poroit nus les maus d'amer
> conter en romanz ne en livre.' (*RR*, 2591–93)

[The God of Love then replied and fully answered my question. [...] 'No more than one could exhaust the entire sea, could one recount all the pains of love in a romance or a book.']

Much later, from Genius, we learn one possible reason for this: the absolute intractability of women, whose resistance to male desire and regulation similarly exceeds the limits of poetic discourse:

> [...] en fame a tant de vice
> que nus ne peut ses meurs parvers
> conter par rimes ne par vers. (*RR*, 16304–06)

[in a woman there is so much vice that no one could ever tell of her perverse habits in rhyme or verse.]

In the course of the poem, in fact, readers of the *Rose* are alternately advised always to believe women ('creez les conme paternostres' [believe them like the 'Our Father'], v. 15728), and never to believe them ('rien ne jure ne ne ment / de fame plus hardiement' [nothing vows or lies more boldly than a woman], vv. 18907–08). So slippery is the feminine that she troubles the very distinction between truth and falsehood.[2] Still, the manifest impossibility of accounting for either desire or the object on which it is focused does not stop Cupid from offering a roadmap to success:

> Or t'ai dit coment n'en quel guise
> amanz doit fere mon servise.
> Or le fai donques, se tu viaus
> de la belle avoir tes aviaus. (*RR*, 2563–66)

[Now I have told you how and in what way a lover should perform my service. Now do it, if you want to take your pleasure with the beautiful one.]

The Lover's attempts to follow Cupid's advice will prove to be far less straightforward than he might have wished. But his travails with the Rose and its guardians, and his efforts to understand the accounts of love and desire expounded by the different characters he encounters, do at least provide rich fodder for poetry.

The desire to express the ineffable nature of love, eros and sexuality is, in fact, every bit as powerfully present in the *Rose* — and every bit as much in danger of being thwarted — as is the desire to experience the pleasures of love themselves. Guillaume's narrator runs into difficulty almost immediately, when he tries to describe the visual appearance of Love personified:

> Li dex d'Amors de la façon
> ne resembloit mie garçon;
> de biauté fist mout a prisier.
> Mes de sa robe deviser
> crien durement qu'encombrer soie. (*RR*, 871–75)

> [In his appearance the God of Love did not resemble a boy; his beauty was greatly to be praised. But I'm really afraid that I'm unable to describe his robe.]

The most Guillaume can tell us about Cupid is that, unlike his avatar in classical poetry, the god's beauty is *not* boyish; whether this means that he is effeminate or that he has the handsome virility of a grown man is not specified. Instead we are given a list of the different species of birds and flowers in which he is clothed, and an admission that his intricately woven robe defies description: poetry cannot produce an integument worthy of love itself.[3] For Jean's narrator, the limitations of language are most poignant in his efforts to describe the personification of Nature — no innocent figure in the *Rose*, for Reason has already informed the Lover that Nature is responsible for the pleasure of sexual climax, and thus for instilling the basic drive whose refinements are dictated by Cupid (*RR*, 4385–90). This is a figure that Love's poet would dearly like to put into words, and his efforts in this regard are as compelling — and every bit as unimaginable — as Nature herself:

> Et por ce que, se je poïsse,
> volantiers au mains l'antandisse,
> voire escrite la vos eüsse
> se je poïsse et je seüsse,
> je meïsmes i ai musé
> tant que tout mon sens i usé
> conme fos et outrecuidiez
> .c. tanz plus que vos ne cuidiez. (*RR*, 16181–88)

> [And since, if I could — I would at least willingly have made the effort — I would have written it up for you, if I could and knew how, I thought about it so much that I exhausted my mind, like an arrogant fool, a hundred times more than you could believe.]

Even Reason cannot keep from trying to describe erotic love, despite her acknowledgment that it cannot be linguistically communicated or learnt:

> Or te demonstreré sanz fable
> chose qui n'est pas demonstrable,
> si savras tantost sanz sciance
> et connoistras sanz connoissance

>   ce qui ne peut estre seü
>   ne demonstré ne conneü. (*RR*, 4249–54)

[Now I will demonstrate, without fables, a thing that cannot be demonstrated, and you will know at once without knowledge, and understand without understanding, that which cannot be known or taught or understood.]

What follows is her long, oxymoronic 'description' of love, adapted — like the disclaimers that precede it — from Alain de Lille's *De planctu naturae* (IX, 1–20 [Meter 5, pp. 149–50]).[4] Unfortunately, Reason was right about one thing: this is not something that can be taught or understood rationally.[5] As the Lover petulantly replies, 'je n'en sai pas plus que devant' [I don't know any more than I did before] (*RR*, 4332).

And yet the *Rose* is supposed to be a poem in which 'l'art d'Amors est tot enclose' [the art of love is completely contained], a claim first made by Guillaume (v. 38) and repeated endlessly in manuscript incipits, explicits and colophons. The 'nota' signs and other marginal annotations in many *Rose* manuscripts indicate that its readers responded to it as a didactic compendium.[6] Some of these annotations do pertain to the Lover's obsession with the Rose, to the allegorical presentation of courtly values, and to the poem's Ovidian adaptations; or at least to passages relevant in some sense to sexual desire or behaviour, such as misogynist diatribes or the exhortation to procreate. But equally often — perhaps even more often — the sententious passages and literary allusions flagged by medieval readers have no obvious connection of any kind to an 'art of love', pertaining instead to such topics as Divine Providence and free will, the origins of government, the abuses of the mendicant friars, the science of optics, and the corrupting effects of material wealth. Superficially, the presence of learned and largely Latinate material in the *Rose* (particularly that of Jean de Meun) can be explained by the university milieu in which he composed the poem, and which likely constituted its first readers.[7] Badel, while cautioning against a facile identification of Jean with the Aristotelian and Averroist doctrines condemned by Etienne Tempier in 1277, readily agrees that the 'subtlety' attributed to the poem in numerous rubrics, colophons and related texts reflects its qualities of being 'difficult' and 'laden with the learning of antiquity'.[8] With its brilliant and often hilarious reworkings, mixtures and parodies of well-known Latin authors, the *Rose* offers a playful and idiosyncratic review of the medieval arts curriculum. Nonetheless, Jean's decision to construct this edifice on the foundations of an allegorical love poem has baffled many a reader. One cannot help but wonder: what is all this seemingly irrelevant material doing in a text that is supposed to be about love?

Critics have both denigrated and marvelled at the 'centrifugal' and 'digressive' nature of Jean's portion of the *Rose*. Both positions are already present in the documents associated with the *querelle* of 1401–02. In an epistle to an unidentified recipient Jean de Montreuil enthuses about the 'misteriorum pondera ponderumque misteria operis illius profundi' [the depths of the mysteries and the mysteries of the depths of this profound work], while Jean Gerson regards the poem as a disordered conglomeration of borrowings from other authors:[9]

car *L'Art d'amour*, laquelle escript Ovide, n'est pas seulement toute enclose ou dit livre, mais sont translatés, assemblés et tirés come a violance et sans propos autres livres plusseurs, tant d'Ovide come des autres.

[for the *Art of Love*, which Ovid wrote, is not the only thing contained in the aforementioned book, but there are many other texts, both by Ovid and by others, translated, assembled, and dragged in violently, for no reason.]

In more modern times, the negative view was perhaps most famously expressed by C. S. Lewis, who echoes Gerson in describing Jean's continuation as a 'huge, dishevelled, violent poem'; he flatly asserts that Jean 'produces chaos. Clumsiness is the characteristic vice of his work. He is a bungler.'[10] Some fifteen years later, Alan Gunn made an equally forceful argument for the poem's unity and its 'essential poetic nature'. Speaking a bit poetically himself, Gunn invites us to read the *Rose* 'as the leisurely opening of a many-petaled and variously tinted rose, as the expansion of a bubble of fancy and thought into a vast and miraculously crystallized iridescent sphere, upon the surface of which are reflected all the multi-colored forms and aspects of love'.[11] And less than two decades after Gunn's work, John Fleming argued for a reassessment of the *Rose* as deriving its unity from an overarching moral agenda.[12] Numerous other critics since that time, however, have positively revelled in the *Rose* — particularly Jean's portion — as a masterfully complex text that refuses to cohere into a single viewpoint. Noah Guynn, for example, describes it as 'hybrid, encyclopedic, polyphonic'; Alastair Minnis terms it 'incorrigibly plural'; and for Sarah Kay it is 'not just dialectical but infinitely slippery'.[13] Daniel Heller-Roazen bases his philosophical reading of the *Rose* on the premise that 'one of the defining characteristics of the two-part romance [...] is that, at each of the fundamental levels of its construction, it presents itself as capable of being otherwise than it is'.[14]

Bewildering though Jean, in particular, may sometimes be, there is a rationale for the seeming chaos of the text. As the Lover gradually comes to realize, he cannot approach the Rose directly, but only tangentially, pretending that he has no real interest in it at all. And the narrator cannot simply transpose the emotional, imaginative and bodily experiences of love, desire, heartbreak and sexual climax into straightforward, expository language. The discourse of desire and sexuality emerges as a deflection from or resistance to some other discourse; or as a kind of undertow, hidden but still discernible in what passes overtly for a discussion of some wholly other topic. The impossibility of speaking openly about erotic desire is implicit in Guillaume's use of allegory and his identification of the erotic poem with the enigmatic imagery of dreams. It is Jean, however, who more fully develops the poetic discourse of desire, pain and pleasure as something nebulous, produced almost as if by accident from the cross-currents of other discourses: digressions into mythology, practical advice about techniques of seduction, tirades about the perfidy of the love object or the travails of marriage, political diatribe, scientific theory, moral admonition, philosophical speculation, theological exposition. All of these discourses are present in the *Rose*, and all of them are in some sense deformed, altered, contaminated. They are contaminated by one another, as in Jean's ceaseless combining, dismantling and recombining of Ovid's *Ars amatoria*, Boethius's *Conso-*

lation of Philosophy, and Alain de Lille's *De planctu Naturae*. Critics have noted, for example, his conflation of Boethius's Philosophy and Alain's Natura in the oddly hybrid figures of both Reason and Nature.[15] Equally striking is his construction of la Vieille as a figure at once Boethian and Ovidian: Philosophy consoling Boethius in prison is reinvented in the guise of a feminized Ovid teaching a male figure of the lady — the imprisoned Bel Acueil — about the tactics and stratagems of love.[16] The kaleidoscopic discourses of the *Rose* are infiltrated by something intangible, an unspoken but powerful energy that circulates through the poem: the ineffable force of desire, struggling to release itself as the drive to jouissance, and holding out the promise of a different sort of knowledge altogether — a knowledge accessed not through language, but through the body.[17]

The purpose of the present study is not to trace the many literary sources and languages at play in the *Rose*. To a large extent, that work has already been done.[18] An exhaustive study of the different discourses that interact within the poem, in any case, is probably no more possible than describing the travails of lovers. My aim instead is to look at some of the ways that a discourse of eros emerges as a kind of 'negative shape': in the gaps between opposing readings that the text both conjures up and denies; in the unspoken implications of its allegorical constructs; in the often unacknowledged web of allusions to prior texts that so richly informs the poem; in the ways that mythological figures, though only explicitly present at one point, operate throughout as an implicit subtext. The *Rose* does transmit considerable knowledge of desire and its attendant pleasures and sorrows, but it does so through poetry: through a language in which what is unspoken is at least as important as what is spoken.[19]

I begin by examining the fictions of authorship and literary creation that both Guillaume and Jean offer the reader, and their treatment of poetry as a vehicle for erotic persuasion and instruction. Chapter 1 focuses on the Ovidian model presented in the *Amores*, tracing the ways that Guillaume develops the notion of erotic discourse as a deflection from a more 'serious' literary form; and then looking at Jean's strategy of pitting this Ovidian stance against the Boethian model of philosophical discourse as a resistance to or deflection from a discourse of desire. Boethius's own persona in the *Consolation* has been analysed as a 'corrected' recasting of the Ovid of the *Amores* — whereas Ovid resists the sage advice of the Tragic Muse, Boethius accepts Philosophy's banishment of elegiac poetry — and Jean exploits this intertextual dynamic for both didactic and comic purposes.[20] Jean also, of course, pits himself against Guillaume, whose work he both continues and rewrites; and I will identify some of the ways in which Jean's continuation frames and recasts the first *Rose*. Chapter 2 examines the myth of Narcissus, both as it is recounted by Ovid, and as it is appropriated by the authors of the *Rose*. Guillaume and Jean, in different ways, exploit aspects of Ovid's tale and its thematic resonances in Boethius (among others) in their treatment of the love poet, the Lover, and the traumatic knowledge that love brings.

Chapters 3 and 4 are devoted to the figure of Orpheus and the tales that he tells. After examining the treatment of Orpheus in both the *Metamorphoses* and the *Consolation of Philosophy*, I will consider the importance of Orpheus, Pygmalion,

Myrrha and Adonis in Jean's *Rose*. I will argue that although Orpheus is explicitly mentioned only once in the *Rose*, in the discourse of Genius, he is implicitly evoked in the debate between the Lover and Reason. It is no surprise to find Orpheus lurking in the intertextual density of Reason's discourse, given the prominence he is accorded by one of Reason's most important literary antecedents, Boethian Philosophy. Not only does Philosophy tell the story of Orpheus's descent to Hell in the strategically placed final meter of Book Three (III, m. 12); but also this passage was frequently expanded in vernacular translations and adaptations of the *Consolation*, reflecting its fascination for medieval readers.[21]

On the one hand, Orpheus and the characters of whom he sings allow Jean to explore both the powers and the limitations of poetic discourse and erotic fantasy; on the other hand, he bears the stigma of pederasty (in Ovid) and of self-absorption born of obsession with an inaccessible love object (in Virgil). And if Reason, like Philosophy, is intent on dissuading the Lover from erroneously clinging to erotic pleasures and the poetry of desire, the Lover himself is more concerned about the implications of renouncing a stance that, in modern parlance, might be described as heterosexual.[22] In this way, the Lover's quest for the Rose develops in resistance not only to the philosophical discourse of Reason, but also to an ever-present undercurrent of autoerotic isolationism, homosocial friendship and homoerotic desire. Orpheus is crucial here, bringing into play a range of Latin authors who told his story or employed him as an iconic figure — Virgil, Ovid, Boethius, Alain de Lille — as well as providing a focal point for an even wider range of intertextual associations, triggered by shared terminology or motifs. The reader's literary knowledge of these standard 'school texts' is exploited, forcing one to consider the different passages that are being combined, and the different literary contexts that are evoked by key phrases or images — a process that, to judge from marginal annotations supplying references to various Latin authors, medieval and early modern readers were often happy to enter into. In the MS Paris, Bibl. de l'Arsenal 3337, for example, numerous citations of Ovid gloss Cupid's teachings and the discourse of Ami, while assorted Latin proverbs and maxims are scattered throughout the manuscript; Bibl. Nat. fr. 1560 is glossed with citations of the Bible, Aristotle, Ovid, Tibullus, Macrobius, Matthew of Vendôme and *Pamphilus*; Bibl. Nat. fr. 24390 contains marginal citations not only of Ovid and of proverbial sayings, but of Gratian's *Decretum*.[23] These and numerous other examples show that early readers of the *Rose* were quite prepared to engage in intertextual readings, sometimes surprisingly wide-ranging, touching on texts that are not explicitly mentioned in the poem as well as those that are. From this commingling of sources, and from the unexpected perspectives implied by their juxtapositions, emerges the unspoken — and perhaps unspeakable — amorous and sexual knowledge promised by the poem.

Chapter 5, finally, examines Jean's use of Virgil. Citations of the *Aeneid* and the *Eclogues*, symmetrically disposed around the final conquest of the Rose, imply a moral critique of the poem's Ovidian teachings. At the same time, the Ovidian tenor of the text tends to appropriate the Virgilian discourse, subjecting it to an erotic reading that, if accepted, cancels out its moral import. It is this capacity to stage conflicting readings of itself — rival voices vying with each other in the citational density of the text — that has enabled the *Rose* to remain a controversial, much-debated poem for well over seven hundred years.

Notes to the Introduction

1. On this passage see Max Grosse, *Das Buch im Roman: Studien zu Buchverweis und Autoritätszitat in altfranzösischen Texten* (Munich: Wilhelm Fink, 1994), pp. 30–33. All citations of the *Rose*, unless specified otherwise, are to the edition by Félix Lecoy, *Le Roman de la Rose*, CFMA, 3 vols (Paris: Champion, 1965–70), and the translations are my own. I will sometimes also refer to the edition by Ernest Langlois, *Le Roman de la Rose*, Société des Anciens Textes Français, 5 vols (Paris: Champion, 1914–24).

2. On the impossibility of accounting for either women or sexual consummation in the *Rose*, see my 'Bodily Peril: Sexuality and the Subversion of Order in Jean de Meun's *Roman de la Rose*', *Modern Language Review*, 95 (2000), 41–61. For an analysis of the contradictory depictions of women in the text and illuminations of the fourteenth-century manuscript Douce 332 of the Bodleian Library, Oxford, see my 'Women and "Woman" in Bodleian MS Douce 332: A Case of "Accidental Meaning"?', in *De la Rose: Texte, image, fortune*, ed. by Catherine Bel and Hermann Braet (Louvain and Paris: Peeters, 2006), pp. 41–58. The whole of MS Douce 332 can be viewed online at the site 'Roman de la Rose Digital Library' <http://romandelarose.org>.

3. For a highly unusual attempt by the illuminator to portray Cupid's robe, see the fifteenth-century MS Ludwig XV 7 at the J. Paul Getty Library, Los Angeles, fols 7^r and 8^r. The images can be viewed online at <http://romandelarose.org>.

4. All references are to *De planctu naturae*, ed. by Nikolaus M. Häring, *Studi Medievali*, 19 (1978), 797–879. Translations are from *The Plaint of Nature: Translation and Commentary*, by James J. Sheridan (Toronto: Pontifical Institute of Medieval Studies, 1980).

5. As Michèle Gally puts it, 'on ne peut expliquer [l'amour] ni le dominer par un discours et un savoir intellectuels et rationnels: le désir est d'un ordre qui échappe à la langue normative de Raison' [one can neither explain nor subjugate love by means of a rational and intellectual discourse and knowledge: desire is of an order that escapes the normative language of Reason], in *L'Intelligence de l'amour d'Ovide à Dante: Arts d'aimer et poésie au Moyen Âge* (Paris: CNRS Éditions, 2005), p. 132.

6. See my 'Medieval Readers of the *Roman de la Rose*: The Evidence of Marginal Notations', *Romance Philology*, 43 (1990), 400–20, and *The 'Romance of the Rose' and Its Medieval Readers: Interpretation, Reception, Manuscript Transmission*, Cambridge Studies in Medieval Literature, 16 (Cambridge: Cambridge University Press, 1993), pp. 47–84; Dieuwke E. Van der Poel, 'Moderne en Middeleeuwse Lezers van de "Roman van de Roos"', in *Wat is Wijsheid? Lekenethiek in de Middelnederlandse letterkunde*, ed. by J. Reynaert (Amsterdam: Prometheus, 1994), pp. 101–15.

7. See Gérard Paré, *Le 'Roman de la Rose' et la scolastique courtoise* (Paris: Vrin; Ottawa: Institut d'Études Médiévales, 1941) and Alastair Minnis, *Magister Amoris: The 'Roman de la Rose' and Vernacular Hermeneutics* (Oxford: Oxford University Press, 2001), for a reading of Jean's *Rose* in the context of Latinate clerical culture. Alain Corbellari outlines the impact of university culture on thirteenth-century vernacular poetry more generally, in *La Voix des clercs: Littérature et savoir universitaire autour des dits du XIIIe siècle*, Publications Romanes et Françaises, 236 (Geneva: Droz, 2005). For an analysis of the marginal 'Nota' signs in the fifteenth-century MS 3 of Senshu University, Tokyo, as possible evidence connecting this particular *Rose* manuscript to a university milieu, see my 'Senshu University MSS 2 and 3 and the *Roman de la Rose* Manuscript Tradition', in *Medieval English Literature: Torches from the Ancient World*, ed. by A. V. C. Schmidt, David Wallace and Tomonori Matsushita (Bern: Peter Lang, forthcoming). Senshu MS 3 can be viewed online at <http://romandelarose.org>. The early fifteenth-century MS 1056 of the Bibliothèque Municipale, Rouen, has a series of scribal annotations that also point to a scholastically trained reader; see Krzysztof Kotuła, 'Deux Méthodes de structuration du texte dans le *Roman de la Rose*: Le Cas des MSS Londres, British Library, Royal 19 B XII et Rouen, Bibliothèque Municipale 1056', *Scriptorium*, 61 (2007), 170–79 (pp. 176–79). Of course the *Rose* did not long remain confined to clerical readers, achieving widespread popularity and notoriety

with aristocratic and bourgeois lay readers and bibliophiles. See Pierre-Yves Badel, *Le 'Roman de la Rose' au XIVe siècle: Étude de la réception de l'œuvre*, Publications Françaises et Romanes, 153 (Geneva: Droz, 1980); and my *'Romance of the Rose'*.

8. Badel, *'Roman de la Rose'*, p. 138; see also pp. 32–54. John Fleming also argues against the identification of Jean de Meun with Averroist doctrines targeted by Tempier, in *The 'Roman de la Rose': A Study in Allegory and Iconography* (Princeton, NJ: Princeton University Press, 1969), pp. 214–18.

9. Montreuil, 'Quo magis magisque' and Gerson, 'Traictié contre le *Ronmant de la Rose*', in *Le Débat sur le Roman de la Rose*, ed. by Eric Hicks, Bibliothèque du XVe Siècle, 43 (Paris: Champion, 1977), pp. 28 and 76.

10. *The Allegory of Love: A Study in Medieval Tradition* (Oxford: Oxford University Press, 1936), pp. 137, 141.

11. *The Mirror of Love: A Reinterpretation of 'The Romance of the Rose'* (Lubbock, TX: Texas Tech Press, 1952), p. 94.

12. See, for example, *'Roman de la Rose'; Reason and the Lover* (Princeton, NJ: Princeton University Press, 1984).

13. Noah Guynn, *Allegory and Sexual Ethics in the High Middle Ages* (New York: Palgrave Macmillan, 2007), p. 137; Minnis, *Magister Amoris*, p. 194, n. 83; Sarah Kay, *The Place of Thought: The Complexity of One in Late Medieval French Didactic Poetry* (Stanford, CA: Stanford University Press, 2001), p. 179. For further reflections on the 'monologism' or 'dialogism' of the *Rose*, see Kay, op. cit., pp. 179–85. Badel proposes a medieval 'lecture discontinue' that did not seek textual unity or a single meaning; see *'Roman de la Rose'*, pp. 135–44.

14. Daniel Heller-Roazen, *Fortune's Faces: The 'Roman de la Rose' and the Poetics of Contingency* (Baltimore, MD: Johns Hopkins University Press, 2003), p. 8.

15. See Sarah Kay, 'Women's Body of Knowledge: Epistemology and Misogyny in the *Romance of the Rose*', in *Framing Medieval Bodies*, ed. by Sarah Kay and Miri Rubin (Manchester: Manchester University Press, 1994), pp. 211–35.

16. See my 'Bodily Peril'; Chauncey Wood, 'La Vieille, Free Love, and Boethius in the *Roman de la Rose*', *Revue de Littérature Comparée*, 51 (1977), 336–42. Douglas Kelly remarks more generally that 'Ovid and Boethius are two distinct mirrors through which Jean refracts Guillaume's dream into new forms and meanings', in *Internal Difference and Meanings in the 'Roman de la Rose'* (Madison: University of Wisconsin Press, 1995), p. 42.

17. In Kay's words: 'The twin themes of the *Rose*, desire and knowledge, are dialectically intertwined so that desire for knowledge generates knowledge of desire, and vice versa' (*Place of Thought*, p. 179).

18. For a survey of the poem's sources, see Ernest Langlois, *Origines et sources du Roman de la Rose* (Paris: Thorin, 1890). Other critical works will be cited in the course of this study, and can also be found by consulting Heather Arden, *The Roman de la Rose: An Annotated Bibliography* (New York and London: Garland, 1993).

19. On the allusive nature of language in the *Rose*, with particular attention to Jean's use of rich rhymes, see David F. Hult, 'Poetry and the Translation of Knowledge in Jean de Meun', in *Poetry, Knowledge and Community in Late Medieval France*, ed. by Rebecca Dixon and Finn E. Sinclair (Cambridge: D. S. Brewer, 2008), pp. 19–41 (35–40). It is an interesting feature of *Rose* criticism that, faced with the poem's lack of moral clarity and the controversies that surround it, critics feel called upon to defend its poetic status. Kelly, for example, emphasizes that 'the *Rose* is not a simple moral treatise' and that 'sophistication is required to appreciate the *Rose* as integumental allegory' (*Internal Difference*, p. 19). Fleming reminds readers that 'Jean de Meun is writing a *poem*, not a philosophical commentary' and that his work is 'more likely to be illuminated by the practice of poets than by that of scholiasts', in 'Jean de Meun and the Ancient Poets', in *Rethinking the 'Romance of the Rose': Text, Image, Reception*, ed. by Kevin Brownlee and Sylvia Huot (Philadelphia: University of Pennsylvania Press, 1992), pp. 81–100 (p. 93).

20. Jo-Marie Claassen, 'Literary Anamnesis: Boethius Remembers Ovid', *Helios*, 34 (2007), 1–35 (pp. 6–8); Anna Crabbe, 'Literary Design in the *De Consolatione Philosophiae*', in *Boethius: His Life, Thought and Influence*, ed. by Margaret Gibson (Oxford: Basil Blackwell, 1981), pp. 237–74 (pp. 244–49).

21. See J. Keith Atkinson and Anna Maria Babbi, eds., *L'Orphée de Boèce au Moyen Âge: Traductions françaises et commentaires latins (XIIe–XIVe siècles)* (Verona: Fiorini, 2000); John Block Friedman, *Orpheus in the Middle Ages* (Cambridge, MA: Harvard University Press, 1970), pp. 86–145.

22. There has been much discussion about the use of the terms 'heterosexual', 'homosexual' and 'homoerotic' in a medieval context. For reflections on the issues involved, see William E. Burgwinkle, *Sodomy, Masculinity, and Law in Medieval Literature: France and England, 1050–1230* (Cambridge: Cambridge University Press, 2004), pp. 1–15; James A. Schultz, 'Heterosexuality as a Threat to Medieval Studies', *Journal of the History of Sexuality*, 15 (2006), 14–29. In employing these terms I do not mean to imply an anachronistic identification of medieval and modern concepts of sexuality and sexual identity, but only to refer to the phenomenon (real or perceived) of sexual desires, acts or relationships between people of the opposite sex or the same sex, respectively.

23. See my *'Romance of the Rose'*, pp. 47–84. MSS Arsenal 3337 and fr. 1560 can be accessed online at <http://romandelarose.org>.

CHAPTER 1

The Desire for Knowledge and the Knowledge of Desire

Models of Poetic Composition in the *Roman de la Rose*

Guillaume de Lorris's characterization of his poem as one in which 'l'ars d'Amors est tote enclose' [the art of love is fully enclosed] (*RR*, 38) has led critics to see it as (among other things) a medieval recasting of Ovid's *Ars amatoria*. And indeed it does contain a lengthy 'art of love', set prominently at the centre of the poem. Though it is far from Ovid's worldly advice about techniques of seduction and the management of erotic liaisons, Cupid's discourse to the Lover does touch on familiar Ovidian motifs: sleepless nights, vigils at the door of the lady, the importance of careful grooming. That Guillaume de Lorris had Ovid's famous *Ars* in mind, and that medieval readers would have made the association, is surely beyond dispute.

Aside from its more discreet exposition of erotic desire, however, Guillaume's *Rose* also differs from the *Ars amatoria* in purporting to present an account of the author's own initiation into love. Though Ovid repeatedly claims amorous experience as the basis for his teachings, it is in the *Amores* that he most fully casts himself in the role of amorous protagonist. And Jean de Meun, in the famous midpoint passage, draws on a passage in the *Amores* — Ovid's elegy for the death of Tibullus (*Am.* III. ix) — to inscribe both Guillaume and himself in a tradition of elegiac love poets. To shed light on the portrayal of poetic identity and erotic desire in both portions of the *Rose*, I would like to consider the importance of the *Amores* as an additional model for Guillaume's *art d'amors*.

'Quod [...] canas, vates, accipe' dixit 'opus!'

In a famous scene at the beginning of the *Amores*, Ovid portrays himself starting out to write a 'serious' epic detailing the assault of the mythical giants on Mount Olympus; but his project is derailed when Cupid intervenes to transform his hexameters into elegiac couplets:[1]

> par erat inferior versus — risisse Cupido
> dicitur atque unum surripuisse pedem. (I.i, 3–4)

[The second verse was equal to the first — but Cupid, they say, with a laugh stole away one foot.]

When the poet complains that Cupid has no business interfering with poetry and that in any case, he has no love object of whom to write, the god swiftly remedies that lack:

> lunavitque genu sinuosum fortiter arcum,
> 'quod' que 'canas, vates, accipe' dixit 'opus!' (I.i, 23–24)

> [Against his knee he stoutly bent moonshape the sinuous bow, and 'Singer,' he said, 'here, take that (which) will be matter for thy song!']

A torrent of love poetry follows, interrupted only briefly when the Tragic Muse endeavours to talk the poet into abandoning his folly and writing something more edifying (III.i). He resists her appeals, however, until the final poem of the collection, where he finally takes his leave of elegy: 'Quaere novum vatem, tenerorum mater Amorum!' [Seek a new bard, mother of tender Loves!] (III.xv, 1).[2]

In a similar vein, we could see Guillaume's narrator as starting out to write a 'serious' work of didactic allegory modelled on the *Somnium Scipionis*. Arguing for the truth-value of his dream, as is well known, Guillaume de Lorris cites Macrobius's commentary on the *Somnium*.[3] In Cicero's narrative, Scipio's dreamer finds himself transported to the Heavens, a place filled with the entrancing music of the spheres. As he continually turns his eyes from the dazzling stars to the tiny point of the earth, Scipio is chastised: '"Quaeso" inquit Africanus, "quousque humi defixa tua mens erit? Nonne aspicis, quae in templa ueneris?"' [Africanus said, 'Tell me, how long will your thoughts be fixed down on the ground? Do you not see into what regions you have come?'] (IV: 9 [17]). In the remainder of the dream, Scipio is exhorted to turn his mind to spiritual concerns, realizing the pettiness of all earthly glory, as well as receiving personal admonitions and political prophecies. Guillaume de Lorris's narrator also begins by going to a place that is patently outside of 'normal reality', to which he is attracted by another sort of natural music — exceptionally beautiful birdsong — and in which he encounters a series of allegorical figures that represent a didactic programme of courtly values.[4] His investigation of the Garden is increasingly inflected by desire, however: not the desire for moral clarity, political knowledge or spiritual redemption, but a sensual desire stoked by the sounds, colours and textures of the Garden. And his intent gaze into the vanishing point of the crystals, unlike that of Scipio onto the earth, is never deflected; instead, he zeroes in on an even tinier point within the already miniaturized image of the Garden — the rosebud — and fixates obsessively on it. At this point the decisive intervention of Cupid turns the poem into a set of love teachings, followed by the narrative of an attempted love quest, in which the poetic narrator is no longer the detached observer but the protagonist.[5]

That this turning point takes place at the Fountain of Narcissus is a fact that has attracted more critical attention than any other aspect of the poem, and I will examine the significance of Narcissus more fully in the next chapter. For now, however, I wish to point out that in mythographic tradition the myth of Narcissus was seen as the vehicle for a moral lesson very similar to the one that Scipio absorbs in his dream. From the vantage point of the Heavens, the earth is revealed to be tiny and insignificant: 'iam ipsa terra ita mihi parua est, ut me imperii nostri, quo quasi punctum eius attingimus, paeniteret' [now the earth itself seemed to me so small that I was ashamed of our empire, which reaches hardly more than a point on its surface] (*Som.* III: 8 [16]). Turning his attention to celestial bodies, Scipio successfully relinquishes his worldly preoccupations. Narcissus, in the Neoplatonic reading elaborated by Plotinus and adapted by medieval mythographers, fails at precisely this task: enamoured of the insubstantial and ephemeral beauty of his own image, he turns his love to the creature rather than the Creator and thus condemns himself to spiritual death.[6] To the extent that Guillaume's opening allusion to Macrobius still operates in the reader's memory by the time we hear about Narcissus, we might expect to read him in a similar light. The narrator's gloss, however, identifies Narcissus as an exemplary warning to those — ladies in particular — who refuse the love not of God, but of their human admirers. Far from admonishing its readers to renounce earthly love, the story of Narcissus as it figures in the *Rose* teaches that such love is to be embraced. This is, after all, a poem designed to present an 'art d'amors', and erotic desire is the context in which its allegory unfolds. Though he begins by citing Scipio's dream as though it were analogous to his own, it is not long before Guillaume's narrator has left Scipio's political, astronomical and spiritual concerns very far behind.

Even given the shift from spirit to body, however, the reader might still expect Guillaume's poem to adhere to a familiar didactic format, in which an authority figure — in this case Cupid — offers his teachings, and then charges the narrator-protagonist with the mission of writing this up for wider circulation. At the very least, one expects the persona to wake up from his dream and reflect, however briefly, on the lessons he has learnt. This kind of trajectory is followed, for example, in the allegorical dream-visions of Alain de Lille, and the tradition continues in the thirteenth- and early fourteenth-century *dits* of such poets as Raoul de Houdenc, Rutebeuf, Baudouin and Jean de Condé, and Watriquet de Couvin.[7] In the *Rose*, however, Cupid applies these teachings directly and pointedly to the narrator himself, who thereby becomes a player within the allegorical world. As others have noted, Guillaume's *Rose* is the earliest example of a text in which the narrator's own subjective experience is the focus of the allegory.[8] And if this is a departure from the norm of didactic allegory, it is very much in keeping with the Ovidian model. When Ovid's authorial persona is shot by Cupid, he becomes a fictional character in his own poetry.[9] Cupid's arrow fills him with desire, but also strangely splits him, so that he now makes himself exemplary, stages himself as the central figure in a book of amorous verse. Guillaume de Lorris likewise portrays himself in an effort to become the exemplary hero of a love story, and by the end of the poem he speaks as the persona of a lyric *complainte*.[10] But since his adventure begins with a reading of edifying images — rather than with the composition of edifying poetry — we need to consider the way in which Guillaume's text presents a model not only of writing, but also of reading inflected by desire, and leading, by implication, to the composition of amorous verse. Here too, the Ovidian example is illuminating.

'Quo [...] ab indice doctus / conposuit casus iste poeta meos?'

Ovid complains, both in the *Amores* and elsewhere, that his readers failed to understand the poems as fiction. Despite the well-known mendacity of poets, with their 'fecunda licentia' [creative wantonness] untouched by 'historica [...] fide' [history's truth] (*Am.* III.xii, 41–42), Ovid's male readers have been so swayed by the eloquence with which he describes the alluring Corinna that they have fallen in love with her themselves:

> quae modo dicta mea est, quam coepi solus amare,
>   cum multis vereor ne sit habenda mihi.
> Fallimur, an nostris innotuit illa libellis?
>   sic erit — ingenio prostitit illa meo. (III.xii, 5–8)

> [She who but now was called my own, whom I began alone to love, must now, I fear, be shared with many. Am I mistaken, or is it my books of verse that have made her known? So will it prove — 'tis my genius has made her common.]

Female readers, in turn, long to see themselves recreated as a poetic mistress, and identify with Corinna:

> et multae per me nomen habere volunt;
>   novi aliquam, quae se circumferat esse Corinnam. (II.xvii, 28–29)

> [And many a fair one wishes for glory through me; I know one who bruits it about she is Corinna.]

Careless readers also confuse the poet Ovid with his amorous protagonist. Berating the distracted poet, the Tragic Muse informs him that his confessional verses have made him the talk of the town, and that people point him out with the cry, 'hic, hic est, quem ferus urit Amor!' [He, he is the one fierce Love is burning up!] (III.i, 20). What the stern Muse sees as gossip, however, the love poet regards as fame; and he throws his lot in once again with the Muse of Elegy, who 'das nostro victurum nomen amori' [gives everlasting glory to my love] (III.i, 65). It is only later, as the jocular mood of the *Amores* gives way to the more urgent tone of the *Tristia*, that Ovid strives to distance himself from his fictional counterpart: 'magnaque pars mendax operum est et ficta meorum: / plus sibi permisit compositore suo' [and most of my work, unreal and fictitious, has allowed itself more licence than its author has had] (*Tr.* II, 355–56).

Ovid imagines the ideal reader of the *Amores* as one who would see his or her own experience mirrored in the poems, implying that they do provide an accurate depiction of erotic experience. At the same time, he teases that reader for believing that Ovid is writing specifically about him:

> miratusque diu 'quo' dicat 'ab indice doctus
>   conposuit casus iste poeta meos?' (*Am.* II.i, 9–10)

> [and, long wondering, (he will) say: 'From what tattler has this poet learned, that he has put in verse my own mishaps?']

In short, Ovid complains — humorously at first, and more plaintively in the post-exile writings — that his readers fail to understand the different kinds of 'truthfulness' or 'realism' contained in poetic fictions.[11] The poems are misread both as autobiography and as a gossipy record of the poet's contemporaries, while the Roman authorities regard them suspiciously as incitement to immoral behaviour. In fact, the poet argues, their truth lies in their ability to capture, through exemplary scenarios, monologue or dialogue, the essence of love as a fundamental human experience.[12]

Nonetheless, Ovid's very protestations serve only to highlight the mimetic response elicited in the readers of love poetry. And his boastful persona takes credit for having refined the raw power of the sex drive into an erotic art, governed by rules and codified into a crafted performance that any reader can adopt. As he comments in the opening lines of the *Remedia amoris*, with reference to the *Ars amatoria*, 'quod nunc ratio est, impetus ante fuit' [what was impulse then is science now] (*Rem.*, 10).[13] The *Ars*, indeed, might be seen as helping its readers to create fictional versions of themselves, while the *Remedia* maps out ways of rewriting the self according to other fictions. Whether or not the reader adopts the strategies recommended by Ovid, he or she will learn that love is a performance, to be continued, altered or halted at will. Overall, Ovid's instructions give his readers an ironic distance from their own love stories, a crucial sense of doubling as they take on the role of lover, rather then merely being driven by an incomprehensible desire. It is the inability to appreciate that ironic gap between construct and reality — between poetic persona and historical author, or between the person and the persona that he or she adopts — that results in a misreading, both of poetry and of oneself.

One could see Guillaume's Lover as a reader who makes the mistake of taking a poem literally, thinking that the personifications and metaphors are entities with whom he can interact. Rather than seeing the Rose as a fiction — the latest form, so to speak, assumed by the elusive Corinna — he mistakes it for an object that he can desire and possess. Rather than understanding the Garden as expressing idealized qualities of love and its ethical underpinnings, he takes it as a concrete instance of those qualities, and strives to make himself an exemplary incarnation of the amorous ideal. He wants no gap between performer and performance, and when Cupid locks up his heart this seals his absolute conformance to the ideal of Love, despite the fact that as yet he barely knows what it is. The need to understand his new role, in fact, is what motivates the Lover to ask Cupid for lessons — in effect, to tell him who he now is. And he receives the ensuing tirade — a didactic poem within the poem — as the script that he must now follow. Since Reason can only urge him to drop the role completely, she is of little help. It will be Ami who will encourage the Lover to open up the crucial gap of artistry in his staging of Cupid's commandments.[14] When Ami instructs the Lover, it is as though the Ovid of the *Amores* was taking lessons from his own *Ars amatoria*.

Even if Cupid and Ami address themselves explicitly to the Lover's situation, their teachings are also aimed at the reader of the poem. The Lover 'reading' first the allegorical imagery of the garden and then the teachings of Cupid, is an image for the (male) reader who, like him, is motivated by desire: a desire for knowledge, both of love and of the amorous dream itself. As the Lover shifts from a desire to see and know the entire garden, to a desire for full sensual knowledge of just one of its flowers, the reader is implicitly encouraged to follow suit. After all, Cupid's teachings take the form of a prescriptive monologue, ostensibly addressed to the Lover but also addressing the reader himself. And it is just as the God of Love begins his sermon that Guillaume plays on the reader's desire with his teasing promises that one is now getting to 'the good part'. The crucial knowledge concealed in the text's poetic figments — beautiful, novel, alluring — is about to be revealed:

> Des or le fet bon escouter,
> s'il est qui le sache conter,
> car la fin dou songe est mout bele
> et la matire en est novele.
> Qui dou songe la fin ora,
> je vos di bien que il porra
> des jeus d'Amors assez aprendre,
> [...]
> La verité, qui est coverte,
> vos sera lores toute overte. (*RR*, 2061–67, 2071–72)

[From here on out it is good to listen to it, if there is someone who can recount it, for the end of the dream is very beautiful, and the material is new. Whoever hears the end of the dream, I tell you, he will be able to learn plenty about the sport of love [...] The truth, which is hidden, will then be fully revealed to you.]

The reader may well look forward to seeing the Lover capture the Rose, but if so he is in for a long wait. At the moment, what is actually offered as an object of readerly desire is knowledge: the pedagogically useful 'fin dou songe', which will grant the reader a clear vision of a 'verité' — that of the 'jeus d'Amors' — that is currently obscured by poetic fictions. What follows in the God of Love's speech is a set of bodily symptoms and forms of behaviour. And as they are entirely phrased in the second-person singular, with a combination of imperative and future-tense verb forms, they have the effect of casting the reader as the hero of a literary fiction that draws on a long tradition of medieval and classical love poetry. Although the reader might approach the poem objectively as an ethical exposition of human love, he might equally see it as a normative mirror of his own inchoate passions, a script as prophetic as the dream itself.

   Yet it is still unclear exactly what the purpose of this knowledge is. Is it meant to increase the would-be lover's success with women? Cupid's disquisition offers little in the way of practical advice. Instead, it focuses almost entirely on the importance of social etiquette — be courteous to all people, honour all women, cultivate a good reputation — and the private torments of desire, such as fevers and chills, obsessive thoughts, nocturnal wanderings and sexual dreams. What the poem offers at this point is not the knowledge needed to fulfil one's desires, but simply knowledge of the workings of desire itself. And the Lover reacts with considerable dismay: *this* is who I now am? What on earth am I supposed to do about it? As he woefully tells his new master: 'Forment en sui espouentez' (*RR*, 2572) [I'm utterly horrified].

'Te mihi materiem felicem in carmina praebe'

Like Ovid, Guillaume exploits these problems of reading and interpretation for comic effect. The second half of his poem, in particular, develops a tension around the uncertainty as to whether the garden is an allegorical construct containing the 'truth' or knowledge offered by the poem, or the setting for an exemplary narrative whose trajectory will be the vehicle by which this knowledge is imparted. Another way of phrasing this dilemma is to ask whether the reader can receive the poem's wisdom merely by meditating on the allegorical figures it presents, or whether it is necessary to explore these qualities and concepts experientially. And if the reader does attempt to model himself on the allegory of the garden, will this mean that its symbolic language has been made real — or that the imitative reader has become a fiction? At the beginning of the poem, the Lover feels a powerful desire to see and know the garden as fully as possible, but at this stage he also retains a certain detachment. He circulates through the garden, noting details both great and small, enumerating species of birds, flowers and trees and delighting in the play of sunlight and shade. He admires the carollers' idyllic existence, commenting: 'Dex! com menoient bone vie! / Fox est qui n'a de tel envie!' [God! what a great life they lead! Whoever doesn't want that is crazy] (*RR*, 1293–94). Yet he makes no effort to join in: 'D'ileques me parti atant, / si m'en alai seus esbatant' [I left that place straightaway, and went cheerfully off by myself] (*RR*, 1299–1300). Perhaps at this stage he is still aware that his ontological status as a human being removes him from any possible engagement with allegorical personifications.

It is at the Fountain of Narcissus that everything changes. There he looks into the crystals and sees, once again, the garden — not of course the actual garden, but an artificial image, a representation of the allegorical construct that he has been exploring. The medium in which this vision appears associates it with the practice of crystal-gazing, a form of prognostication that would have been known, at least in legendary form, to Guillaume and his contemporaries.[15] The image at which the Lover gazes is thus a miniaturized version of the prophetic dream itself. The text is ambiguous as to whether he sees himself or not, describing his action at the fountain with the verbs *[re]mirer* and *se mirer*, both of which designate the action of gazing intently, while the latter can additionally have the reflexive sense of gazing at oneself.[16] Still, it is possible to distinguish the way that each term respectively is deployed throughout the passage, with the former used for the act of gazing at some object, while the latter carries strong implications of seeing oneself.[17] The narrator refers to the '.ii. pierres de cristal / qu'a grant entente *remirai*' [two crystal stones that *I gazed at* intently], and to Narcissus, who '*mira* sa face et ses ieuz vers' [*beheld* his face and his grey eyes], before then issuing the more general warning that 'Qui en ce miroër *se mire* / ne puet avoir garant ne mire' [he who *gazes (at himself)* in that mirror can have no help or cure] (*RR*, 1536–37, 1571, 1573–74, emphasis mine). The latter, presumably, refers to anyone who, like Narcissus, beholds their own reflection in the fountain — it is, after all, described as a mirror. This distinction would make sense of the narrator's rueful comment on his own actions, implying that it was not the mere fact of looking into the fountain that caused his downfall, but specifically the fact of gazing upon his own image:

> Adès me plot a demorer
> a la fontaine *remirer*
> et as cristaus, qui me mostroient
> mil choses qui entor estoient.
> Mes de fort eure *m'i miré*. (*RR*, 1601–05, emphasis mine)

[Then it pleased me to stop there, *gazing* into the fountain and the crystals, which showed me a thousand things that were all around. But woe is me that *I gazed (at myself) in there*.]

As the Lover as beholds the garden with himself in it, a shift takes place. As imaged in the crystals, the Lover suddenly does have the same status as the allegorical personifications. Both they and he are pictured as inhabitants of the garden, and suddenly he sees himself as one of their number. I do not mean to argue that Guillaume portrays the Lover as falling in love with himself; indeed, his interpretation of Narcissus stresses not self-absorption or self-love, but desire for an unattainable object. But as the Lover gazes into the fountain, he sees himself as a fictional character in an allegorical poem, and is simultaneously filled with the desire that will determine his narrative role in that very poem from that moment on.[18]

It is also at this point that the Lover discovers that while he thought he was moving about the garden as a detached observer, he was actually being followed by its presiding deity, and in that sense was already committed to narrative engagement. The narrator informed the reader of this development as soon as the Lover, withdrawing from the carol, embarked on his tour: 'Li dex d'Amors tantost de loing / me prist a sivre l'arc ou poing' [the God of Love at once began to follow me at a distance, bow in hand] (*RR*, 1311–12). The Lover himself, however, is blissfully unaware: 'Je, cui de ce ne fu noient, / m'alai adez esbanoiant' [I, who knew nothing of this, went along enjoying myself] (*RR*, 1315–16). What exactly should we make of this menacing gaze which, from beyond the Lover's view, now stalks him through the garden?

Cupid's earlier description presents him as, in effect, a concentrated and even more artful version of the garden itself. He is clothed in a 'robe de floreites' [robe of flowers] in which an ornate pattern of birds and beasts is 'de toutes parz / portrete, et ovree de flors / par diversité de colors' [depicted and worked all over with flowers of different colours] (*RR*, 877, 882–84). Like the garden, Love's robe is a complete assemblage of every kind of flower — 'Nule flor en esté ne nest / qui n'i fust' [no flower is born in summer that was not there] (*RR*, 887–88) — and they appear in every possible colour. He is also covered with birds of different species: 'de papegaus, de rosigniaus, / de kalendres et de mesanges' [parrots, nightingales, larks and tits] (*RR*, 900–01). The Lover imagines himself to be walking freely through the garden, observing its every detail. But since he is being followed surreptitiously by Cupid — a walking mass of flowers and songbirds — it is as though the garden itself, embodied in the force of desire, is watching him even more intently. The fountain offers an even more concentrated version of the garden. And as the Lover gazes into its crystals, he is simultaneously in the garden; staring at an image of the entire garden and himself in it; and being stared at by a personification of that very garden. The respective gazes of Cupid and the Lover interlock, and it is at this point that he is infused with the desire that underwrites the garden's very existence. It remains only for him to select a love object, and he too can be an exemplary lover. Were he only a bit less naïve, we might imagine him courting the Rose in the words of Ovid: 'te mihi materiem felicem in carmina praebe' [give me yourself as happy matter for my songs] (*Am.* I.iii, 19).[19]

But if the Lover is inserting himself into a poetic fiction, what sort of fiction is it — and how does it impart an 'art of love' to its readers? Ovid's persona focuses his desire on an attractive woman; but Guillaume's Lover turns his attentions to a rosebud. The ensuing poem of love for what remains a resolutely botanical object cannot be taken at face value as an exemplary love story, from which the reader might learn how to court a garden flower. Yet its allegorical quality is often strained by the pressures of a narrative that vacillates between allegory and exemplarity. As the poem proceeds, there is a growing tension as to whether its actors are universal qualities, whose visual appearance and attributes are to be decoded into an ethical discourse on love, or characters whose behaviour makes them particular instances of those qualities, which we learn about by observing the narrative action. These two sorts of didacticism coexist uneasily, surrounding the expository presentation of the rules and behavioural codes of love at the heart of the text. It has frequently been noted that as we pass from the description of iconic allegorical personifications in the first half, to exemplary narrative in the second, the status of the allegorical figures themselves becomes increasingly problematic.[20] Dangier, for example, relaxes under the influence of the Lover's soothing promises, and is accused by Honte of behaving too much like Bel Acueil (*RR*, 3677–80). Yet while this may be unorthodox behaviour for the allegorical personification of Dangier, it is entirely natural if he is a character with whom the Lover can negotiate, susceptible to flattery and charm. Bel Acueil, in turn, should be the very embodiment of courtesy and favourable reception, as even Honte herself admits. And yet as the Lover presses for the Rose, Bel Acueil resembles Dangier with his forceful refusal: 'Frere, vos beez / a ce qui ne puet avenir' [brother, you desire something that can never be] (*RR*, 2892–93). Venus even accuses him of being 'dangereus' (*RR*, 3425). But again, if Bel Acueil is a person rather than a personification, his shifting positions are understandable. Bel Acueil's masculine gender poses little problem too, as long as he is merely a static representation of courtly receptivity. But the more he emerges as a narrative figure and the object of the Lover's affections, the more problematic his gender becomes. Medieval artists sometimes depicted Bel Acueil as female, while certain others show him as variously male or female. John Fleming has interpreted this latter technique as an effort to clarify the way that his allegorical role shifts between being a guardian of the Rose, interested in friendship but not in sexual contact, and being much more closely identified with the lady herself as object of desire; while Simon Gaunt sees it as reflecting a playful appreciation of the hetero- and homoerotic innuendos of the text.[21] Other critics have offered divergent readings of Bel Acueil that variously seek to develop, neutralize or deny any homoerotic implications of his character.[22] If nothing else, it is clear that the allegorical personae invented by Guillaume and further manipulated by Jean are far from straightforward in their meaning.

The interpenetration of personification allegory and exemplary narrative thus becomes increasingly troubled, as the Lover's efforts to live out the literary paradigm he has just absorbed lead to stalemate and despair. Lacking the ironic detachment that enabled Ovid to bid an airy farewell to the Elegiac Muse at the end of the *Amores*, Guillaume's narrator never does stand back from his story to offer the promised exposition of the dream. His voice merges seamlessly with that of his protagonist, culminating in a long lament that trails off into silence. But then, Cupid did say that the many-splendoured experience of love can never be expressed in words (*RR*, 2591–93). The *Rose* itself is clearly no exception to this rule.

'Cist avra le romanz si chier / qu'il le voudra tout parfenir'

If the impossibility of voicing and analysing desire explains the silences, paradoxes and inconclusiveness of Guillaume's poem, it assumes a different role in Jean de Meun's continuation, which one might see as eagerly rising to the challenge. No poem can adequately cover the kaleidoscopic, ineffable and unspeakable experience of erotic love? Perhaps not, but Jean gives it his best shot, producing a poem that has proved to be every bit as inexhaustible as its putative subject matter. He offers several ways of understanding the 'art d'amors' enclosed in Guillaume's text. Two of these might be characterized as primarily Ovidian, or indeed as corresponding to the inaccurate readings that Ovid both boasted and complained of.[23] Recording its author's experience of love, the poem will serve as instruction and inspiration for others. The object of the poet's affections will be moved to a favourable response; more generally, male and female readers alike will be initiated into the mysteries of love. This characterization of the *Rose* is articulated most explicitly in the discourses of Ami and the God of Love.

In his much longer and more explicitly Ovidian reappearance in Jean's portion of the poem, Ami comments regretfully that poetry is unlikely to be of much value in courtship (*RR*, 8307–16; cf. *Ars*, II, 272–86). There is, however, one kind of fictional discourse that Ami does recommend as a seduction ploy:

> Si li doit faindre noveaus songes,
> touz farsiz de plesanz mençonges,
> que, quant vient au soir qu'il se couche
> touz seus en sa chambre en sa couche,
> avis li est, quant il someille,
> car poi i dort et mout i veille,
> qu'i l'ait entre ses braz tenue
> trestoute nuit trestoute nue. (*RR*, 9853–60)

[He should make up novel dreams, full of pleasant lies, claiming that when he goes to bed alone at night, in his bedroom, it seems to him when he dozes off — for he sleeps little, and is mostly awake — that he holds her all night long, completely naked, in his arms.]

In effect, Ami advises the Lover to become a poet; while *faindre* can refer to any sort of dissemblance, it is also the word typically used to refer to the production of poetic fictions and fables in Old French. Building on Guillaume's dedication of his poem to a lady, Jean implies that the original *Rose* may simply have been concocted to seduce 'cele qui [...] / doit estre Rose clamee' [she who should be called Rose] (*RR*, 42–44). Acting on the advice of his savvy companion, 'Guillaume de Lorris' created an account of a fictional erotic dream detailing his desire for a beautiful love object, and his despair at not being able to access her; his gloss on the Narcissus story warns her pointedly about the fate meted out to unmerciful ladies.

Such a reading casts Guillaume's references to Macrobius, and the truth-claims made for the dream, in an especially ironic light. As has often been pointed out, the use of Macrobius to authorize the truth-value of an erotic dream is dubious, given that Macrobius himself identifies such dreams with the *insomnium* or nightmare, devoid of higher meaning or value (Book I, cap. 3.3–6).[24] Still more damningly, this view is repeated by Cupid, who characterizes the dreams of lovers as 'pensee delitable / ou il n'a que mençonge et fable' [delightful fantasies where there is nothing but lies and fables] (*RR*, 4233–34). Even Cupid himself agrees that in dreams sent by him, 'n'a se fables non et mençonges' [there is nothing but fables and lies] (*RR*, 2) — a salutary correction, perhaps, to the Lover-narrator's faith in the prophetic nature and pedagogical value of his dream. Reason indirectly hints at the dangers of misinterpreting the admonitory potential of the erotic dream when she regales the Lover with the example of Croesus, who so woefully failed to understand his own dream.[25] A blanket dismissal of *all* dreams, with explicit reference both to the dream of Scipio and to erotic dreams of the kind narrated by Guillaume de Lorris, will be argued still more forcefully by Nature, who considers such things as 'trufle et mançonge' [silliness and lies] (*RR*, 18333).[26]

If we read Ami's suggestion back into Guillaume's poem, however, we might suspect not only that a dream of this kind falls short of the visions and revelations favoured by Macrobius, or at the very least that it is dangerously subject to misinterpretation, but indeed that it never happened in the first place. If such a reading casts doubts on the 'Macrobian' qualities of the *Rose*, it highlights its Ovidian roots; as Peter Allen states, what Ovid's poetry teaches above all is 'how to appreciate and to create a world of fiction'.[27] If the Lover's dream cannot be redeemed in the Macrobian sense of divine revelation, it may nonetheless contain a truth of the sort that Reason identifies with poetry:

> car en leur geus et en leur fables
> gisent deliz mout profitables
> souz cui leur pensees covrirent,
> quant le voir des fables vestirent. (*RR*, 7145–48)

> [for the pleasures found in their playful constructs and fables, with which they cover their ideas, are very profitable, when they clothe the truth with fables.]

Of course, since Ami himself, like Cupid, Reason and Nature, is a character in the very dream that may never have taken place and whose meaning is problematic even if it did, there results one of those logical conundra so characteristic of the *Rose*. But then it is unlikely that any reader of the *Rose* ever believed that the historical Guillaume de Lorris really did have the dream that he describes — still less, that it might have included everything in Jean's continuation. Paradoxically, reducing the dream to a fictional device for attracting the attentions of a lady offers greater truth-value than the claims made for the dream itself. And collectively, these passages also force us to consider ways that the dreams of lovers, like the lies of poets with which they are so intimately connected, may have an epistemological value as vehicles for knowledge despite their inherent fictionality.[28]

Be that as it may, Ami's comments suggest a view of Guillaume's *Rose* as designed to inspire reciprocal love in female love objects. The knowledge it transmits beneath its fictional surface is a very personal one, concerning the passion of the poet for his dedicatee. Like Ovid's female readers, eager to be the next Corinna, Guillaume's female reader(s) will aspire to the role of the Rose. But if Jean invites us to imagine that Guillaume's *Rose* was composed with those ends in mind, he also questions the legitimacy of such an endeavour. Once Guillaume's persona has constructed his erotic allegory and made his plea for amorous mercy, consolation is offered not by 'Lady Rose' but by a distinctly unsympathetic Lady Reason. As I have already noted earlier, Reason's role as an opponent to love finds precedent in the Tragic Muse's confrontation with Ovid's persona in the *Amores*. Tragedy's chastisement of Ovid even takes place in a setting that has a fortuitous resemblance to the *vergier* in which Reason confronts the Lover: a sylvan grove graced with a fountain and resounding with birdsong (*Am.* III.i, 1–4). But the heavily Boethian substance of Reason's discourse also reveals her as an avatar of Lady Philosophy.[29] As David Hult has pointed out, Jean attaches Guillaume's *Rose* to his own in such as way as to imply that Reason's second intervention arises in response not merely to the Lover's lamentations at the beginning of Jean's continuation, but to his 'recital', as narrator, of the entirety of Guillaume's poem.[30] The Lover's stance as Jean's continuation opens therefore parallels not only that of Ovid's persona when, as author of Books I and II of the *Amores*, he is accosted by the Tragic Muse; but also that of Boethius's persona, who is caught by Philosophy in the act of composing the mournful poem with which the *Consolation* opens. And just as Philosophy angrily chases the 'poeticas Musas' [Muses of poetry] from Boethius's side, branding them as 'scenicas meretriculas' [theatrical tarts] (*CP* I, pr. 1, 26, 29), so Reason encourages the Lover to shun Cupid: 'te lo que hors l'an boutes' [I advise you to kick him right out] (*RR*, 4581).[31] Reason's appearance as the Lover bemoans his fate acts as a hinge, joining the Ovidian and the Boethian intertexts that so richly inform the *Rose*. Like Ovid in thrall to Elegy, and like Boethius consorting with the Muses, Guillaume's narrator — having now become Jean's protagonist — is sharply rebuked for his foolish desires and frivolous verses.[32] Like the Tragic Muse, however, Reason does propose an alternative literary path for the Lover; I will return to this point below.

Unlike Boethius, the Lover is unmoved by the arguments of rational wisdom. He soon returns to the Ovidian terrain of Ami, and then to a second encounter with Cupid. The discourse of Cupid at the midpoint of the conjoined *Rose*, which revisits his lecture at the midpoint of Guillaume's own poem, famously includes a lengthy discussion of the authorship and composition of the *Rose*.[33] Cupid envisages the poem not as a tool of seduction, but as a detailed instruction manual in amorous rules and techniques: a 'Miroër aus Amoreus' [Mirror of Lovers] (*RR*, 10621). It is important to note that the composition of the text is the principal reason Cupid gives for helping 'Guillaume de Lorris' attain the Rose. Though he does speak of assuaging the Lover's pain and reuniting him with Bel Acueil, he justifies this by

citing 'Guillaume's' loyal service, which will culminate in the composition of the
Rose:

> car por ma grace deserver
> doit il conmancier le romant
> ou seront mis tuit mi conmant. (*RR*, 10518–20)

> [For in order to earn my favours, he must begin the romance where all my
> commandments will be placed.]

Within the fictional narrative framework this might imply that it requires an
experienced lover to write such a poem: having brought the quest to fruition, he will
know all the tricks, and be able to transmit them to others. Such an interpretation
would be in keeping with the Ovidian model initiated by Guillaume de Lorris.
Later protestations notwithstanding, in the *Ars* Ovid disavows any assistance from
Apollo or the Muses, insisting that 'Usus opus movet hoc' [experience inspires
this work] (*Ars* I, 29). Beyond that, however, it is easy to elide the amorous and
poetic projects, and to see the attainment of the Rose purely in terms of attaining
the knowledge needed to write the poem. In exhorting his troops, Cupid places
greatest emphasis on the poetic project:

> Et se por lui ne vos prioie,
> certes prier vos en devroie
> au mains por Jehan alegier,
> qu'il escrive plus de legier. (*RR*, 10631–34)

> [And if I wasn't begging you for his sake, certainly I would have to beg you at
> least to alleviate Jean's task, so that he can write more easily.]

The Rose, in other words, affords not — or not only — sexual pleasure but also
sexual knowledge. Unfortunately, the figure who actually falls in love with, pursues
and eventually 'has' the Rose will only live long enough after waking up to record
the opening scenes of his elaborate 'dream'; but luckily, another poet will eventually
take up the task of completing the story. And the more comprehensive the dream
— the greater its exposure of the range of erotic pains and pleasures — the more
easily Jean will be able to write a correspondingly comprehensive poem.

   In this sense the Rose may be seen as embodying the aspirations of an entire
poetic tradition. In a replay of Ovid's elegy on the death of Tibullus (*Am.* III.ix),
Cupid cites a series of poets who served him well until they died. Guillaume is
only the latest in a long line of poet-lovers who, in a manner of speaking, were all
engaged in the effort to capture the mysterious Rose; Jean is soon to follow. When
Jean's lover-narrator, making his way to the Rose in the poem's exciting conclusion,
boasts that 'g'i passai touz li prumiers' [I was the very first to pass there] (*RR*, 21627),
he is casting a jocular eye back to this very passage. Jean himself is, after all, the
second poet to love and pursue this very Rose, or indeed the third if we consider
the intervening anonymous author of the short continuation.[34] His insistence on
being the first to attain it is a lewd comment on the importance attached by men
to female virginity, but it also reminds us of the long poetic tradition in which the
quest for the Rose is inscribed. Perhaps, indeed, Jean was the first to consummate
desire for the Rose, and for all that it stands for; certainly his poetic depiction

of sexual intercourse is unlike anything in any of his Latin forbears. And his sly speculations about subsequent lovers of the Rose — 'Ne sai s'il fist puis d'avantages / autant aus autres conme a moi' [I don't know if he later granted as much to others as he did to me] (*RR*, 21630–31) — lays down a challenge to future poets to match his virtuosity. Many indeed would tread the terrain of that poem, though again we might conclude that few, if any, managed to enjoy the Rose in quite the same way.

In different ways, then, Jean invites us to see the *Rose* as a poem designed both to instruct and to persuade its readers; like Ovid's poetry, it will convert men and woman alike to the great game of love. Cupid's wish for a truly comprehensive 'art of love' defines the *Rose* as part of a poetic tradition, subordinating the pleasure of possessing the Rose to the task of committing this experience to poetry. But these are not the only contexts in which the poem can be read. Literary processes — reading, glossing, writing — are of even greater prominence at other points in Jean's poem: most notably, the discourses of Genius and Reason.

Both bodily and literary models are present in Genius's metaphors of writing as sexual intercourse. In his infamous sermon to Love's troops, Genius roundly condemns those who 'ne daignent la main metre / en tables pour escrivre letre' [do not deign to lift a hand and write on the tablets] (*RR*, 19533–34), and reminds his audience that Nature supplied them with 'greffes' [styluses] so that 'tuit i fussent escrivain' [they would all be writers] (*RR*, 19605). Taking Genius at his word would imply a view of the Lover as writing his way to the Rose: a vision remarkably similar to that outlined by Cupid, except that for Genius the writing is metaphorical, and the ultimate goal is not the composition of a poetic text, but the begetting of an heir. Indeed, Genius envisions numerous begettings, reminding his audience that sexual activity should be habitual and not an isolated occurrence. That is, the *Rose* stages the sexual quest in a manner that naturalizes both the driving force of desire and its heterosexual and reproductive aspects, while at the same time identifying it metaphorically with the production of the poem itself. The Rose, or its attainment, implies jouissance; but as long as it remains simply that — a much desired but unimaginable bliss that lies beyond the pleasures on display in Deduit's garden — it can never be attained, at least not in poetry. As long as orgasmic climax is the object of the quest, writing will only serve to prolong that quest forever, as is confirmed in the long list of poets who have failed to exhaust the subject: Gallus, Catullus, Tibullus, Ovid, and now, most recently, Guillaume de Lorris.[35] How does one portray, in the symbolic codes of poetry, the ultimate, absolute consummation of a desire that can know no further reaches?

In Genius's view, however, orgasmic climax itself is only a means to the true end of procreation — itself not really an 'end' either, but more of a stopgap measure in the ceaseless battle against extinction; and that is something to which writing is well suited.[36] The protracted eroticism that is fostered in the garden is entirely focused on the pleasure that lies in the tension between desire and resistance. The strangely androgynous or indeed asexual nature of the Rose — at once phallic and feminine, yet also merely a flower — suggests that gender is hardly even a factor in this equation. Homo- or hetero-erotic desire alike will flourish in this environment, producing an endless flow of poetic enticements, refusals and lamentations. Genius not only condemns the focus on erotic *oisiveté* at the expense of procreative *labour*;[37] he also detaches writing from any association with the poetry of desire and identifies it with continuity of lineage. Literary, epistemological and sexual readings of the Rose come together if we read the poem's conclusion both as a depiction of (at least potentially) procreative sex, and as an act of literary procreation.[38]

If Genius proposes a metaphoric 'writing' as the task of the Lover, it could also be said that Jean, as an authorial figure distinct from the Lover, writes his way to the Rose in the most literal possible sense. Jean himself claims that all he has done is to 'reciter' what had already been said by Latin authors before him (*RR*, 15204). This is an interesting way of defining the erotic quest — or more properly, the poetic record of the erotic quest — and takes us back to an earlier moment in Jean's continuation: the confrontation of Reason and the Lover. Refusing to play Boethius to Reason's Philosophy, the Lover in effect undoes Boethius's undoing of the Ovidian model, as if forcing Reason back into the role of the Tragic Muse who tries, unsuccessfully, to talk Ovid out of writing still more love poetry. Though Ovid spurns the Tragic Muse, he does so with the promise of a more serious work yet to come:

> 'exiguum vati concede, Tragoedia, tempus!
>   tu labor aeternus; quod petit illa, breve est.'
> Mota dedit veniam — teneri properentur Amores,
>   dum vacat; a tergo grandius urguet opus! (*Am.* III.i, 67–70)

> [Indulge thy bard a short space, O Tragedy! A labour eternal art thou; what she asks is but brief. She was moved, and granted my prayer — let the tender Loves come hasting, while I am free; close after me presses a greater task!]

In a similar vein, after a lengthy debate about not only love but also language, obscenity and poetic integuments, the Lover promises Reason that he will eventually get around to the literary study that she recommends, albeit after his own fashion:

> Mes des poetes les sentences,
> les fables et les methaphores
> ne bé je pas a gloser ores.
> Mes se ja puis estre gueriz
> et li services m'iert meriz
> don si grant guerredon atens,
> bien les gloseré a tens,
> au mains ce que m'en afferra. (*RR*, 7160–67)

> [But as for the wise sayings of the poets, the fables and metaphors, I have no wish to gloss them right now. But if I can ever be healed, and my service is acknowledged, for which I expect such great reward, I will certainly gloss them in due course, at least, insofar as it pertains to my situation.]

Perhaps, then, the *Rose* is the fruit of that labour: a learned treatise on all aspects of love and desire, in which plenty of Latin authors are indeed glossed — often to within an inch of their lives.[39] The *Rose* may not be quite what Reason had in mind; it is certainly unlike the text produced by Boethius when his own poetic lamentation was interrupted by Philosophy. But Jean's continuation does represent a radical rethinking of Guillaume's poem, and a movement well beyond its more modest boundaries.

Two 'Ovidian' models operate in Jean's poem, then; but they seem to be at cross-purposes. Ami's proposal suggests that the *Rose* is but a ploy to enhance its author's reputation with the ladies — another means to the end of an ever-deferred sexual consummation. The Lover's promise to Reason, however, implies that the fulfilment of erotic desire is a necessary pre-condition to any serious literary work; sexual knowledge itself will be the lens through which he will read a corpus of poetic, philosophical and scientific texts. Cupid's exhortation of his troops further qualifies the Lover's literary plans by portraying sexual fulfilment as necessary for the initial poetic composition, in which the Lover himself records his own erotic history; Jean de Meun, more obscurely, will benefit from Guillaume's experience while drawing his own knowledge directly from Cupid himself. To which model does the *Rose* most clearly conform? Are we meant to read it as a learned work produced in the aftermath of youthful folly? Or — as Christine de Pizan would later claim — is the *Testament* actually the 'serious', moralizing poem to which Jean eventually turned his hand, while the *Rose* can only be identified with the frivolous juvenilia for which he apologizes in that later work?[40] Equally uncertain is the didactic import of the poem itself. Is the *Rose* an *Ars* or a *Remedia* of love? Does it console lovers with philosophical wisdom, or with helpful advice for amorous success — or perhaps by offering them a quasi-pornographic means of experiencing erotic pleasure without having to worry about the troublesome female at all? This very fact of opposing discourses, of personae who offer conflicting readings of the text within which they reside, and of inscribed readers whose interpretations are both encouraged and mocked, is a feature that links the *Rose* to both its Ovidian and its Boethian models.[41]

We recall that in Cupid's eyes, attaining the Rose will endow 'Guillaume de Lorris' with the knowledge and authority needed to begin work on a poem designed to contain the entire 'art d'amors'. Cupid earlier asserted that this was an impossible task, perhaps because of his own commitment to the indefinite prolongation of desire, and his relative indifference to its consummation. In this particular case, however, he takes an interest in bringing desire to a climax and, one assumes, a cessation, so that the experience can be complete. The closure of desire, in turn, will allow for a completeness and closure to the text of desire: for once, the experience of love will have been taken all the way to the endpoint, and the satiated Lover can concentrate on writing it up. Small wonder, perhaps, that one who had exhausted the depths of desire might lack the energy fully to record the experience, or that the true cessation of desire could come only with death. Foiled yet again, as the 'art d'amors' languishes unfinished, Cupid must wait for another poet to take up the task; but this time he selects one whose work will not be based on that formative erotic experience. It will be the *Rose*, rather than the Rose, that inflames the young Jean's desires: 'Cist avra le romanz si chier / qu'il le voudra tout parfenir' [he will so love the romance that he will want to complete it] (*RR*, 1554–55). And rather than shooting the poet with one of his infamous arrows, Cupid has something else in mind:

> je l'afubleré de mes eles
> et li chanteré notes teles
> que, puis qu'il sera hors d'enfance,
> endoctrinez de ma sciance,
> si fleütera noz paroles
> par carrefors et par escoles. (*RR*, 10607–12)

[I will cloak him with my wings and sing him such songs that, by the time he leaves childhood, indoctrinated with my teachings, he will broadcast our words in the streets and in schools.]

Jean will be imbued with love's teachings while still in the cradle; for him, the composition of love poetry will be primary, not a detour or deflection from some other discourse, some other body of knowledge. The difficulties inherent in writing the definitive study of a topic that is by definition inexhaustible might mean that this encyclopaedic art of love can *only* be written by a poet who has approached it through an intellectual knowledge of love's 'sciance', rather than a bodily knowledge of erotic desire. As portrayed in the *Rose*, Jean's poetic undertaking was never disrupted by Cupid's arrows. If it had been, presumably he too would have been launched into the inexhaustible and inexpressible trajectory that both delighted and defeated all of Cupid's other poets.

Notes to Chapter 1

1. Quotations and translations of Ovidian texts are from the following editions: *Amores*, ed. and trans. by Grant Showerman and G. P. Goold, Loeb Classical Library (Cambridge, MA and London: Harvard University Press, 1977); *Ars amatoria*, in *The Art of Love and Other Poems*, ed. and trans. by J. H. Mozley, Loeb Classical Library (Cambridge, MA: Harvard University Press; London: William Heinemann, 1969); *Metamorphoses*, ed. and trans. by Frank Justus Miller, Loeb Classical Library, 2 vols (Cambridge, MA: Harvard University Press; London: William Heinemann, 1971); *Remedia amoris*, in *The Art of Love and Other Poems*, ed. and trans. by J. H. Mozley, Loeb Classical Library (Cambridge, MA: Harvard University Press; London: William Heinemann, 1969).

2. On the opening poems in each of the three books of the *Amores*, see Leslie Cahoon, 'A Program for Betrayal: Ovidian *Nequitia* in *Amores* 1.1, 2.1, and 3.1', *Helios*, n.s. 12 (1985), 29–39. On *Amores* III.i, see Giancarlo Mazzoli, 'Tragedia vs. Elegia: Genesi e rifrazioni d'una "scena" metapoetica ovidiana (Am. 3,1)', in *Ovid: Werk und Wirkung. Festgabe für Michael von Albrecht zum 65. Geburtstag*, ed. by Werner Schubert, 2 vols (Frankfurt-am-Main: Peter Lang, 1999), I, 137–55. On the persona of Ovid's love poetry, see also John M. Fyler, '*Omnia Vincit Amor*: Incongruity and the Limitations of Structure in Ovid's Elegiac Poetry', *The Classical Journal*, 66 (1971), 196–203; Michael Stapleton, *Harmful Eloquence: Ovid's Amores from Antiquity to Shakespeare* (Ann Arbor: University of Michigan Press, 1996), pp. 1–37.

3. On Guillaume's dream and its possible affinities with Macrobius's teachings, see Jean Dornbush, '"Songes est senefiance": Macrobius and Guillaume de Lorris' *Roman de la Rose*', in *Translatio Studii: Essays by His Students in Honor of Karl D. Uitti for His Sixty-fifth Birthday*, ed. by Renate Blumenfeld-Kosinski, Kevin Brownlee, Mary B. Speer and Lori J. Walters (Amsterdam: Rodopi, 2000), pp. 105–16; David F. Hult, *Self-fulfilling Prophecies: Readership and Authority in the First 'Roman de la Rose'* (Cambridge: Cambridge University Press, 1986), pp. 114–26; Rupert T. Pickens, '*Somnium* and Interpretation in Guillaume de Lorris', *Symposium*, 29 (1974), 175–86; Armand Strubel, 'Écriture du songe et mise en œuvre de la "senefiance" dans le *Roman de la Rose* de Guillaume de Lorris', in *Études sur le 'Roman de la Rose' de Guillaume de Lorris*, ed. by Jean Dufournet (Paris: Champion, 1984), pp. 145–79. Quotations and translations of the *Somnium* are from Cicero, *Laelius, on Friendship (Laelius De amicitia) and the Dream of Scipio (Somnium*

Scipionis), ed. and trans. by J. G. F. Powell (Warminster: Aris and Phillips, 1990); citations of Macrobius's commentary refer to Macrobio, *Commento al Sogno di Scipione*, ed. by Moreno Neri (Milan: Bompiani, 2007). Citations of the *Somnium* are identified, as in Powell's edition, both by Powell's own subdivisions of the text and by the passage's numeration within the standard edition of Cicero's *De re publica*.

4. The parallel as well as the contrast between Scipio's dream and that of the Lover is highlighted in the fifteenth-century MS Ludwig XV 7 at the J. Paul Getty Library, Los Angeles, by a double miniature that portrays Scipio's dream on the left, and the Lover's on the right (fol. 1ʳ). The image is accessible online at <http://romandelarose.org>.

5. An important difference between the *Rose* and the *Amores* is that Ovid is already a poet when he encounters Cupid, who intervenes in the very act of writing. Guillaume's dreamer is not explicitly acting as a poet when he is targeted by the God of Love. The experience is, however, one that — according to the fictional framework of the text — resulted in Guillaume's persona becoming a poet.

6. See Frederick Goldin, *The Mirror of Narcissus in the Courtly Love Lyric* (Ithaca, NY: Cornell University Press, 1967), pp. 6–7; Hult, *Self-fulfilling Prophecies*, pp. 294–95.

7. On Watriquet's use of allegory, see my 'The Writer's Mirror: Watriquet de Couvin and the Development of the Author-Centered Book', in *Across Boundaries: The Book in Culture and Commerce*, ed. by Bill Bell, Philip Bennett and Jonquil Bevan (Winchester: St Paul's Bibliographies; New Castle, DE: Oak Knoll Press, 2000), pp. 29–46; Michel Zink, 'The Allegorical Poem as Interior Memoir', trans. by Margaret Miner and Kevin Brownlee, *Yale French Studies*, 70 (1986), 100–26. On the allegorical journey to the 'other world' in medieval French texts, see Fabienne Pomel, *Les Voies de l'au-delà et l'essor de l'allégorie au Moyen Âge* (Paris: Champion, 2001). On the impact of the *Rose* itself on medieval French dream-vision poetry, see Badel, *'Roman de la Rose'*, pp. 331–53.

8. Hans-Robert Jauss, 'La Transformation de la forme allégorique entre 1180 et 1240: d'Alain de Lille à Guillaume de Lorris', *L'Humanisme médiévale dans les littératures romanes du XIIe au XIVe siècle*, ed. by Anthime Fourrier (Paris: Klincksieck, 1964), pp. 107–44.; Zink, 'Allegorical Poem'.

9. See Cahoon, 'Program', p. 34.

10. I have argued elsewhere for the movement from didactic narrative to lyricism in Guillaume's *Rose*; see my *From Song to Book: The Poetics of Writing in Old French Lyric and Lyrical Narrative Poetry* (Ithaca, NY: Cornell University Press, 1987), pp. 86–90. For a detailed analysis that also takes this view, as well as arguing for the integrity of Guillaume's poem as a finished text, see Hult, *Self-fulfilling Prophecies*, pp. 208–62. See also Claire Nouvet, 'A Reversing Mirror: Guillaume de Lorris's *Romance of the Rose*', in *Translatio Studii: Essays by His Students in Honor of Karl D. Uitti for His Sixty-fifth Birthday*, ed. by Kevin Brownlee, Renate Blumenfeld-Kosinski, Mary B. Speer and Lori J. Walters (Amsterdam and Atlanta, GA: Rodopi, 2000), pp. 189–205; Leslie C. Brook, 'Learning, Experience and Narrative Stance in Guillaume de Lorris's *Rose*', *French Studies*, 49 (1995), 129–41. Some critics, however, see Guillaume's poem as moving from lyric to narrative; see Michelle A. Freeman, 'Problems in Romance Composition: Ovid, Chrétien de Troyes, and the *Romance of the Rose*', *Romance Philology*, 30 (1976), 158–68 (p. 167); Joan Kessler, 'La Quête amoureuse et poétique: La Fontaine de Narcisse dans le *Roman de la Rose*', *Romanic Review*, 73 (1982), 133–46 (p. 137).

11. Peter L. Allen argues that medieval treatises on love, following the Ovidian example, can be seen as 'arts of reading', in 'Ars Amandi, Ars Legendi: Love Poetry and Literary Theory in Ovid, Andreas Capellanus, and Jean de Meun', *Exemplaria*, 1 (1989), 181–205.

12. For a survey of deception, concealment and revelation as recurring motifs in Ovid's love poetry, with particular attention to the *Amores*, see Alison Sharrock, 'Ovid and the Discourses of Love: The Amatory Works', in *The Cambridge Companion to Ovid*, ed. by Philip Hardie (Cambridge: Cambridge University Press, 2002), pp. 150–62.

13. Fyler notes the irony of this claim in 'Omnia Vincit Amor', pp. 201–03. Marilynn Desmond states that Ovid 'mocks the assumption [...] that sexuality can be regulated by law', in *Ovid's Art and the Wife of Bath: The Ethics of Erotic Violence* (Ithaca, NY: Cornell University Press, 2006), p. 36.

14. Ami's recommendation of duplicity is greatly expanded by Jean de Meun, but his role in shaping the Lover's behaviour is already clear in Guillaume's poem.

15. For a discussion of the crystals from the perspective of medieval theories of vision and imagination, see Suzanne Conklin Akbari, *Seeing through the Veil: Optical Theory and Medieval Allegory* (Toronto: University of Toronto Press, 2004), pp. 55–66; Claire Nouvet, 'An Allegorical Mirror: The Pool of Narcissus in Guillaume de Lorris' *Romance of the Rose*', *Romanic Review*, 91 (2000), 353–65. Though crystal-gazing was officially suspect, it was known in medieval Europe; see, for example, John of Salisbury's account of his own experiences in *Policraticus* II, 28.

16. Karl D. Uitti argues against a reflexive sense for 'se mirer', stressing that 'The Lover-protagonist did *not* gaze upon himself in the crystals' (emphasis his), in '"Cele... [qui] doit estre Rose clamee" (Rose, vv. 40–44): Guillaume's Intentionality', in *Rethinking the 'Romance of the Rose': Text, Image, Reception*, ed. by Kevin Brownlee and Sylvia Huot (Philadelphia: University of Pennsylvania Press, 1992), pp. 39–64 (p. 62, n. 23). Sarah Kay, 'Love in a Mirror: An Aspect of the Imagery of Bernart de Ventadorn', *Medium Aevum*, 52 (1983), 272–85, makes a similar argument (pp. 272–75). Numerous other critics, however, have understood the Lover to be seeing himself, as Narcissus did.

17. Goldin interprets the distinction between 'mirer' and 'se mirer' in this manner; see *Mirror*, p. 57. In his view, what the Lover sees in the crystals is 'an idealized image of what he is to become' (p. 59).

18. Emmanuèle Baumgartner offers a similar reading: 'Avant d'être miroir, la fontaine de Narcisse est d'abord texte [...] Au rêveur de lire le texte, de le revivifier' [Before being a mirror, the fountain of Narcissus is a text [...] It is for the dreamer to read the text, to bring it back to life], in 'L'Absente de tous bouquets', in *Études sur le 'Roman de la Rose' de Guillaume de Lorris*, ed. by Jean Dufournet (Paris: Champion, 1984), pp. 37–52 (pp. 50–51). Philip Hardie characterizes Ovid's Narcissus as 'a figure for the desiring reader, caught between the intellectual understanding that texts are just texts, [...] and the desire to believe in the reality of the textual world', in *Ovid's Poetics of Illusion* (Cambridge: Cambridge University Press, 2002), p. 147.

19. Cahoon, 'Program', notes that in Ovid's *Amores*, poetry first engenders desire, then creates the fictional object of that desire.

20. See Kay, *The 'Romance of the Rose'*, Critical Guides to French Texts (London: Grant and Cutler, 1995), pp. 26–27; Noah Guynn, 'Le Roman de la Rose', in *The Cambridge Companion to Medieval French Literature*, ed. by Simon Gaunt and Sarah Kay (Cambridge: Cambridge University Press, 2008), pp. 48–62 (p. 51); Eric Hicks, 'Donner à voir: Guillaume de Lorris or the Impossible Romance', trans. by Deborah S. Reisinger and Christine Reno, *Yale French Studies*, 95 (1999), 65–80; Hult, *Self-fulfilling Prophecies*, pp. 238–45. On Guillaume's personifications see also Eric Hicks, 'La Mise en roman des formes allégoriques: Hypostase et récit chez Guillaume de Lorris', in *Études sur le 'Roman de la Rose' de Guillaume de Lorris*, ed. by Jean Dufournet (Paris: Champion, 1984), pp. 53–82; Stephen G. Nichols, 'Parler, penser, voir: Le Roman de la Rose et l'étrange: "Lucarne" du manuscrit au XIIIe siècle', *Littérature*, 130 (June 2003), 97–114 (pp. 111–13); Carolynn Van Dyke, *The Fiction of Truth: Structures of Meaning in Narrative and Dramatic Allegory* (Ithaca, NY: Cornell University Press, 1985), pp. 75–80. For a similar discussion of Jean's personification of Reason, see Donald W. Rowe, 'Reson in Jean's *Roman de la Rose*: Modes of Characterization and Dimensions of Meaning', *Mediaevalia*, 10 (1988), 97–126 (pp. 104–06). Akbari, *Seeing*, argues that confusion arises between Bel Acueil and Dangiers 'not because they have developed into independent personae or characters, but rather because they are each a reflection of the narcissistic self' (p. 106); in her view, it is only in Jean's continuation that 'the personification's status as a fictional character is privileged' (p. 107).

21. Fleming, '*Roman de la Rose*'; Simon Gaunt, 'Bel Acueil and the Improper Allegory of the *Romance of the Rose*,' *New Medieval Literatures*, 2 (1998), 65–93. Both Fleming and Gaunt provide illustrations depicting Bel Acueil in his or her various guises.

22. See Ellen L. Friedrich, 'When a Rose Is Not a Rose: Homoerotic Emblems in the *Roman de la Rose*', in *Gender Transgressions: Crossing the Normative Boundary in Old French Literature*, ed. by Karen J. Taylor (New York: Garland, 1998), pp. 21–43; Hult, *Self-fulfilling Prophecies*, pp. 244–45; Minnis, *Magister Amoris*, pp. 203–07; Jo Ann Hoeppner Moran, 'Literature and the Medieval Historian', *Medieval Perspectives*, 10 (1995), 49–66; Michel Zink, 'Bel-Accueil le travesti du *Roman de la Rose* de Guillaume de Lorris et Jean de Meun à "Lucidor" de Hugo von Hofmannsthal', *Littérature*, 47 (October 1982), 31–40.

23. On Jean's use of Ovid, see Thérèse Bouché, 'Ovide et Jean de Meun', *Le Moyen Âge*, 83 (1977), 71–87; Langlois, *Origines*, pp. 119–27.

24. On this point see n. 3 above.

25. See Eric Jager, 'Reading the *Roman* Inside Out: The Dream of Croesus as a *Caveat Lector*', *Medium Aevum*, 58 (1988), 67–74.

26. On the mendacity or truthfulness of dreams throughout the *Rose*, see Kevin Brownlee, 'Pygmalion, Mimesis, and the Multiple Endings of the *Roman de la Rose*', *Yale French Studies*, 95 (1999), 193–211.

27. *The Art of Love: Amatory Fiction from Ovid to the 'Romance of the Rose'* (Philadelphia: University of Pennsylvania Press, 1992), p. 37.

28. For a discussion of ancient and medieval views of both dreams and poetic fictions as resisting categorization as either true or false, and the relevance of this tradition for the *Rose*, see Heller-Roazen, *Fortune's Faces*, pp. 34–42.

29. In a much-noted passage, Reason even comments that a vernacular translation of the *Consolation of Philosophy* would be of great use in educating the laity (*RR*, 5006–10). The *Consolation* had already been translated into Old French more than once by the time Jean wrote these lines, but he may already have been laying the groundwork for his own translation.

30. 'Closed Quotations: The Speaking Voice in the *Roman de la Rose*', *Yale French Studies*, 67 (1984), 248–69.

31. I cite Boethius, *Consolation of Philosophy*, ed. by E. K. Rand, trans. by S. J. Tester, Loeb Classical Library (Cambridge, MA and London: Harvard University Press, 1973).

32. See Michael D. Cherniss, 'Jean de Meun's Reson and Boethius', *Romance Notes*, 16 (1975), 678–85 (p. 681); Christophe Lucken, 'Les Muses de Fortune: Boèce, le *Roman de la Rose* et Charles d'Orléans', in *La Fortune: Thèmes, représentations, discours*, ed. by Yasmina Foehr-Janssens and Emmanuelle Métry (Geneva: Droz, 2003), pp. 145–75 (pp. 152–56); Kelly, *Internal Difference*, p. 38; Karl August Ott, 'Jean de Meun und Boethius: Über Aufbau und Quellen des Rosenromans', in *Philologische Studien: Gedenkschrift für Richard Kienast*, ed. by Ute Schwab and Elfriede Stutz (Heidelberg: Winter, 1978), pp. 193–227.

33. See Gally, *Intelligence*, pp. 34–39; Guynn, *Allegory*, pp. 144–47; Heller-Roazen, *Fortune's Faces*, pp. 49–53; Hult, *Self-fulfilling Prophecies*, pp. 10–25, 100–04; my *'Romance of the Rose'*, pp. 52–53, 89–91; Virginie Minet-Mahy, 'Le Songe: De la mort de l'auteur à la naissance du lecteur', in *Le Rêve médiéval*, ed. by Alain Corbellari and Jean-Yves Tilliette, Recherches et Rencontres, 25 (Geneva: Droz, 2007), pp. 193–220 (pp. 197–202); Karl D. Uitti, 'From *Clerc* to *Poète*: The Relevance of the *Romance of the Rose* to Machaut's World', in *Machaut's World: Science and Art in the Fourteenth Century*, ed. by Madeleine Pelner Cosman and Bruce Chandler (= *Annals of the New York Academy of Sciences*, 314 (1978)), 209–16. On rubrication and illustration of this passage, of the break between the two parts of the poem, and of the poem's authors in general, see Herman Braet, 'Du portrait d'auteur dans le *Roman de la Rose*', in *Medieval Manuscripts in Transition: Tradition and Creative Recycling*, ed. by Geert H. M. Claassens and Werner Verbeke (Louvain: Louvain University Press, 2006), pp. 81–99; Hult, *Self-fulfilling Prophecies*, 74–89; Lori Walters, 'Author Portraits and Textual Demarcation in Manuscripts of the *Romance of the Rose*', in *Rethinking the 'Romance of the Rose': Text, Image, Reception*, ed. by Kevin Brownlee and Sylvia Huot (Philadelphia: University of Pennsylvania Press, 1992), pp. 359–73.

34. The seventy-six line anonymous continuation of Guillaume's poem, in which the Lover spends a blissful night with the Rose, appears in at least six manuscripts. It is edited by Langlois as a note to v. 4058 of his edition of the *Rose*. See my *'Romance of the Rose'*, pp. 242–44.

35. Even Jean seems in no hurry to complete the quest; as Badel remarks, 'Écrire pourrait bien avoir été pour Jean de Meun un plaisir dont le *Roman de la Rose* retarde manifestement l'achèvement' [Writing could well have been, for Jean de Meun, a pleasure whose fulfilment was manifestly delayed by the *Roman de la Rose*] (*'Roman de la Rose'*, p. 54).

36. Speaking of both Jean and Ovid, Allen asserts that the poetic text not only seduces the reader, but 'even reproduces itself through him or her by making the reader a maker of interpretations, meanings, and further texts. Reading and writing [...] are thus amatory, erotic, and even procreative experiences', in *Art of Love*, p. 108.

37. In an implicit criticism of Guillaume's *vergier*, whose gatekeeper is Oiseuse, Genius notes that

'Nature por estre *oiseuses* / ne leur avoit por ce prestees' [it wasn't for *idleness* that Nature loaned them] the 'greffes' and 'tables' of sexual procreation (*RR*, 19602–03, emphasis mine). And in his exhortation to Love's troops to engage in procreative sexual activity, he urges: 'Pensez de Nature honorer, / servez la par bien *laborer*' [remember to honour Nature, serve her by *working hard*] (*RR*, 20607–08, emphasis mine).

38. The Lover's claim to have mingled his seed with that of the Rose, thereby making the rosebud 'ellargir et estandre' [expand and widen] (*RR*, 21697–700), is read as an allusion to pregnancy by Thomas D. Hill, 'Narcissus, Pygmalion, and the Castration of Saturn: Two Mythographical Themes in the *Roman de la Rose*', *Studies in Philology*, 71 (1974), 404–26; and Fleming, *Reason and the Lover*, pp. 17–24. It is seen not as pregnancy but as arousal by Kelly, *Internal Difference*, p. 71; and Gaunt, 'Bel Acueil', pp. 71–72. My present view is that the passage probably refers not (or not only) to pregnancy or arousal, but — building on the Lover's lewd comments about wide, well-trodden roads and narrow pathways — to the 'expansion' of the vagina in the act of defloration. Still, seed is sown; and the intervention of Nature and Genius, with their heterosexual procreative agenda, is an integral part of the process by which the Lover reaches his goal.

39. On this promise for a 'delayed gloss', see Renate Blumenfeld-Kosinski, 'Overt and Covert: Amorous and Interpretive Strategies in the *Roman de la Rose*', *Romania*, 111 (1990), 432–53.

40. This point is debated by Pierre Col ('Aprés ce que', pp. 89–112 (p. 95)) and Christine ('Pour ce que entendement', pp. 115–50 (p. 121)); see Hicks, ed., *Débat*. I do not, of course, mean to imply that any of the models constructed within the poem should be understood as historically accurate explanations of its composition.

41. On the ironic and double-edged tone of Ovid's poetry, see Allen, 'Ars Amandi'; Cahoon, 'Program'; Hardie, *Ovid's Poetics*; Stapleton, *Harmful Eloquence*. On opposing discourses in the *Consolation of Philosophy*, see Sarah Kay, 'Touching Singularity: Consolation, Philosophy, and Poetry in the French *dit*', in *The Erotics of Consolation: Desire and Distance in the Late Middle Ages*, ed. by Catherine E. Léglu and Stephen J. Milner (New York: Palgrave Macmillan, 2008), pp. 21–38. With regard to the *Rose*, Minet-Mahy notes: 'La fiction du songe accentue l'expression du décalage, de la distance du soi à soi. Cette modalité du texte donne l'occasion de forger des figures d'auteur et des sujets de texte variés' [The fiction of the dream accentuates the expression of displacement, of the distance of self from self. This aspect of the text allows for the construction of figures of the author and of various textual subjects] ('Songe', p. 218).

CHAPTER 2

Desire, Knowledge and Self-Knowledge

Narcissus and the *Rose*

The Narcissus episode in the *Rose* has been the object of extensive critical discussion. That it plays a central role in the dynamics of Guillaume's poem is, in fact, one of the few things that critics of all persuasions agree on. Just what that role is, however, has been much disputed.[1] For some, Narcissus is a model for the Lover, revealing the spiritual bankruptcy of his foolish passion; for others, Narcissus is the Lover's foil, representing the potential dangers that the courtly protagonist will overcome.[2] Narcissus has also been seen as a figure for the reader, who may either succumb to the deceptive allure of the text, or see beyond it to discover a morally edifying critique of desire.[3] Even the narrator's gloss on the Narcissus story — a warning to ladies not to let their lovers pine away — has been seen by some as an appropriate reading in the courtly context, and by others as a sign of the Lover's confusion.[4] If nothing else, then, it is clear that Narcissus must be taken into account in any reading of the *Rose*. His story revolves around problems of desire, knowledge and interpretation; as such, it plays an important role in integrating the Ovidian-Boethian nexus that operates in both parts of the poem. This chapter will use Narcissus as a lens through which to analyse the ways that both authors of the *Rose* explore the link between erotic desire and knowledge — particularly self-knowledge.

'Qui sibi notus erit, solus sapienter amabit'

In the course of her meandering meditations on the problem of sin and free will, freely adapted from the *Consolation of Philosophy*, Jean's Nature comments that 'cil seus aime sagement / qui se connoit antierement' (*RR*, 17761–62) [he alone loves wisely, who knows himself fully]. On the face of it, there is nothing extraordinary about this statement. The passage in which it appears is an amplification of Philosophy's comments on the importance of self-knowledge:

> Humanae quippe naturae ista condicio est ut tum tantum ceteris rebus cum se cognoscit excellat, eadem tamen infra bestias redigatur, si se nosse desierit. Nam ceteris animantibus sese ignorare naturae est; hominibus vitio venit. (*CP* II, pr. 5)

> [For the nature of man is such that he is better than other things only when he knows himself, and yet if he ceases to know himself he is made lower than the brutes. For it is natural for other animals not to have this self-knowledge; in man it is a fault.]

Nature follows the Boethian text, albeit with considerable digressions, as she compares the human capacity for self-knowledge to the lack thereof in mere beasts. Ignorance is no vice in creatures that were never endowed with a rational faculty in the first place, but in humans or angels, the loss of self-knowledge is directly linked to sin: 's'el se mesconnoit conme nice, / cist defauz li vient de son vice' [if he foolishly fails to know himself, this defect results from his vice] (*RR*, 17835–36). For Nature, self-knowledge is essential to the exercise of free will. Only by accepting responsibility for their actions will people be able to free themselves from sin: 'car bien retrere s'an peüssent, / mes qu'il san plus se conneüssent' [for they could easily withdraw from it if they simply knew themselves] (*RR*, 17757–58). It is this salutary self-knowledge that allows human sinners to seek God's forgiveness and to recover the mutual love between creature and Creator: 'Leur createur lors reclamassent, / qui les amast se il l'amassent' [they should supplicate their creator, who would love them if they loved him] (*RR*, 17759–60).

There would seem, then, to be nothing in Nature's discussion of these matters that is not in line with both philosophical tradition and Christian doctrine. And yet her sententious couplet has a source that is far removed from Boethius; indeed, the connection that Nature establishes between self-knowledge and love is absent from Philosophy's teachings. In Ovid's *Ars amatoria*, however, the god Apollo makes a cameo appearance in which he advises Ovid to lead his disciples to the Delphic temple, with its proclamation 'Know thyself': 'Qui sibi notus erit, solus sapienter amabit' [Only he who knows himself will love with wisdom] (*Ars* II, 501). Neither spiritual awakening nor moral self-scrutiny is Apollo's concern as, decked with the laurel branches of his own first love, he addresses the 'lascivi [...] praeceptor Amoris' [preceptor of wanton love] (497). Instead, he offers advice about the importance of knowing, and exploiting, one's bodily features:

> Cui faciem natura dedit, spectetur ab illa;
> Cui color est, umero saepe patente cubet;
> Qui sermone placet, taciturna silentia vitet;
> Qui canit arte, canat; qui bibit arte, bibat. (*Ars* II, 503–06)

[Let him to whom nature has given beauty be looked at for that; he who has a fair skin, let him oft lie with shoulder visible; let him who pleases by his talk break the still silence; who sings well, let him sing; who drinks well, let him drink.]

This emphasis on manipulating personal appearance is essential to Ovid's art of love, and is prominent in the *Rose* as well. Guillaume's Cupid stresses the importance of personal hygiene and elegant clothing; while in Jean's continuation, Ami and la Vieille dispense advice about all aspects of bodily appearance, from clothing and make-up, to highlighting one's best physical features, to the language of gestures, laughter and tears.

Since we have already been through the Ovidian teachings of Cupid, Ami and la Vieille by the time we encounter Nature's comments on self-knowledge and love, we might wonder just how we are supposed to take this: in bodily terms, or spiritual ones? Just what sort of love is Nature referring to? The contrast with animals is interesting; as Nature explains,

> San faille toutes bestes mues,
> d'antandemant vuides et nues,
> se mesconnoissent par nature. (*RR*, 17763–65)

[Without fail all dumb animals, barren and devoid of intellect, naturally lack self-knowledge.]

Nature's ensuing discussion first applies the lack of animal rationality to their inability to work cooperatively in resistance to human domination, as though she were less concerned with their lack of self-knowledge than with their incapacity to know one another. Ultimately, however, she does contrast this natural ignorance with the rationality and self-consciousness of higher beings, the loss of which has such tragic consequences. The implication is that dumb beasts, unlike humans and angels, are incapable of virtuous behaviour but also, crucially, of sin. As she then explains at greater length — moving from Boethian Philosophy to Alain de Lille's Natura as her model — neither the elements, nor the heavenly bodies, nor any of the plants or animals, give her cause for concern; all perform their allotted tasks without resistance. People alone, with their capacity for both rationality and irrationality, commit sins against God and Nature.

So far, so good; but what has this to do with love? On the one hand, animals do not know themselves, and they do not love; they merely mate. Only people are capable of accessing the spectrum of loves, which lead from lust, conjugal love and friendship to the mystical love of God. At the same time, animals also mate unproblematically, fulfilling the natural imperative to procreate. They do not participate in the eroticism that, from a strict moral perspective, blights human sexuality. With its emphasis on desire, on pleasure, and indeed on the pleasures of desire itself, human eroticism runs counter to the procreative project — or at least, this is a message that emerges from the discourses of Nature and Genius. Spiritual self-knowledge, as expounded by Philosophy to Boethius, allows for detachment from earthly desire, to be replaced with the desire for wisdom, and ultimately union with God. In the sub-lunar realm of Nature, ethical self-knowledge grants access to a sober form of love, regulated by the sacrament of marriage and oriented towards procreation rather than pleasure.

The bodily self-knowledge of Ovid, however, opens up a space for erotic play. And by instructing both men and women in the *Ars amatoria*, he ensures that the conquest will never be simple; both parties will be skilled at arousing and prolonging desire. Bringing in the figures of Reason and Nature, both of whom are a curious blend of Alain's Natura and Boethian Philosophy, Jean places them in implicit dialogue with the Ovidianism of Ami and la Vieille. The shock waves from this textual confrontation reorient the poem's 'art d'amors'. The relationship between desire and knowledge — the different kinds of love and desire that are associated with different forms of knowledge and discourse — is examined repeatedly, often in unexpected ways. As an initial example of the relevance of Narcissus to this thematic nexus, I begin with a fourteenth-century reading that, surprising though it may seem, links the passage discussed above to Narcissus.

'Si se non noverit'

The example I wish to focus on is taken from a fourteenth-century index, or 'finding-aid', attached to a copy of the *Rose* (Paris, Bibl. Mazarine, MS 3874).[5] The medieval indexer made no effort to organize his long series of entries into any kind of over-arching order; one has the distinct impression, in fact, that they simply appear in the order in which he thought of them, the fruits of his constant reading and rereading of the *Rose*. For this very reason, they are an invaluable record of one medieval reader's engagement with this text. The indexer created an entry for Nature's comments on animal irrationality; and interestingly, he placed it between two allusions to the Narcissus story. The first refers to Guillaume's well-known Narcissus episode; the other, to Reason's evocation of Echo's distress at being rejected in love:

> ¶ De narchisus. xi. *[v. 1437]*
> ¶ Que bestes mues n'ont mie entendement. vi^{xx} + vi. *[v. 17763]*
> ¶ Que pucheles refusees sont dolentes. xlii. *[vv. 5804–05]*
>> (Paris, Bibl. Mazarine, MS 3874, fol. 1v)

> [About Narcissus [...] That dumb animals have no rational faculty [...] That maidens who are spurned are sorrowful.]

At first glance, the irrationality of animals seems completely irrelevant to the story of Narcissus. But as we have seen, Nature's comment is followed only two lines later by its corollary: animals, lacking the rational faculty, 'se mesconnoissent' (v. 17765). Our indexer evidently understood this incapacity as referring to self-knowledge, and associated it with Narcissus's own disastrous experience of self-recognition. In the *Metamorphoses*, after all, the story of Narcissus is introduced as a tale about the fatal impact of self-knowledge:

> Narcissumque vocat. de quo consultus, an esset
> tempora maturae visurus longa senectae,
> fatidicus vates 'si se non noverit' inquit. (*Met.* III, 346–48)

> [She named him Narcissus. When asked whether this child would live to reach well-ripened age, the seer replied: 'If he ne'er know himself.']

Seen as a figure that resisted self-knowledge and was unable to benefit from it when it was finally thrust upon him, Narcissus contributes to a moral reading of the *Rose*. The Lover conceived his passion for the Rose at the Fountain of Narcissus, and from a moral perspective, is now alienated from his rational faculty and blinded by self-deception. Reason, in the third index entry noted above, urges the Lover to direct his love to her, inviting him to gaze into the mirror of her face — 'Regarde chi quelle fourme a / Et te mire en mon cler visage' [Behold here its form, and gaze (at yourself?) in my bright face] — and warning him to avoid repeating the error made by Narcissus in drawing the wrath of a woman scorned: 'Trop sont dolantes et confuses / Puceles qui sont refusees' [Maidens who are spurned are all too sorrowful and humiliated] (Bibl. Maz. MS 3874, fol. 43^r; cf *RR*, vv. 5784–5808).[6] Reason in effect offers the Lover the ethical self-knowledge that Narcissus lacked. As Nature explains, to know oneself is to understand one's rational faculty as the image of

God, to see one's sins, to repent and be reconciled with the Creator. The Lover, however, resists any such insight into his condition; as he explains, Cupid holds such sway over his thoughts that 'par l'une des oreilles giete / quan que Reson en l'autre boute' [whatever Reason puts in one ear, he throws out the other] (*RR*, 4610–11). The Lover's wilful resistance replays not only Narcissus's initial misrecognition, but also his irrational persistence in love even after he has, in fact, recognized himself: that is, a failure of self-knowledge.

I would suggest that the indexer of the Mazarine manuscript understood the references to Narcissus in this way, and therefore saw a connection to the Narcissus theme when he encountered Nature's discussion of self-knowledge and love. In the first entry noted above, he considers the exemplary story of Narcissus. He associates it with a passage that links self-knowledge to wise and ethical love, and identifies a lack of self-knowledge with bestial irrationality. And he then applies this double lesson back onto the Lover, connecting it all up with the passage in which Reason implicitly urges the Lover to know himself, avoiding the dangers of Narcissan self-deception. Idiosyncratic though this particular reading may be, it alerts us to the importance of Narcissus, not just for Guillaume's portrayal of the onset of love, but for the entire *Rose*. In order to pursue these intertwined themes of desire and self-knowledge, we must take a closer look at this important mythological tale: not only as it is told by Guillaume, but also in Guillaume's most likely source, the *Metamorphoses*.

'Inopem me copia fecit'

For a medieval reader, Narcissus is a parodic inversion of the moral trope of self-knowledge as salvific — a notion familiar to all readers of Boethius. Philosophy, in her efforts to heal the grieving Boethius, diagnoses the temporary suspension of self-knowledge as the root cause of his unhappiness:

> 'Iam scio,' inquit, 'morbi tui aliam vel maximam causam; quid ipse sis, nosse desisti [...] Nam quoniam tui oblivione confunderis, et exsulem te et exspoliatum propriis bonis esse doluisti.' (*CP* I, pr. 6)

> ['Now I know,' she said, 'that other, more serious cause of your sickness: you have forgotten what you are [...] For because you are wandering, forgetful of your real self, you grieve that you are an exile and stripped of your goods.']

Philosophy equates self-knowledge with the Neoplatonic doctrine that the goods of Fortune can be neither possessed nor lost, and are irrelevant to the attainment of happiness. True wealth — true happiness — is identified with the treasures of the soul. As Philosophy argues:

> Quid igitur o mortales extra petitis intra vos positam felicitatem? Error vos inscitiaque confundit. (II, pr. 4)

> [Why then do you mortals look outside for happiness when it is really to be found within yourselves? Error and ignorance confuse you.]

Seeking material wealth and worldly success only impoverishes the soul, bringing as it does the relentless drive to acquire even more — since no amount of worldly goods can ever bring happiness — as well as the ever-present fear of loss. 'Fugare credo indigentiam copia quaeritis,' says Philosophy severely. 'Atqui hoc vobis in contrarium cedit' [You want, I think, to banish need with plenty. But yet you achieve exactly the opposite] (II, pr. 5).

Narcissus's tormented cry, upon realizing that his love object is himself, bears an uncanny resemblance to the moralizing discourse that consoled the unhappy Boethius: 'quod cupio mecum est: inopem me copia fecit' [What I desire, I have; the very abundance of my riches beggars me] (*Met.* III, 466). If we separate this line into its two halves, we find what seems to be an encapsulation of Philosophy's doctrine: your desires can be fulfilled by looking within yourself, where you already possess all that you could ever really wish for. As for an abundance of earthly riches, or 'copia', they will only rob you of happiness, making you poor and needy. The irony of Narcissus's self-analysis, however, is that he makes no distinction between the 'quod cupio' of the first half, and the 'copia' of the second. Far from being consoled at discovering that he already *possesses* the means of satisfying the soul's true desire, Narcissus is distraught at the discovery that he can no longer look forward to the experience of *acquiring* this good in an endless cycle of desire, pleasure and loss. Erotic desire must, by its very nature, be routed through an 'other' with whom one can experience the bliss of contact, without suffering the permanence of a true union that would put an end both to the prolongation of desire, and to the prospect of repeated, if always ephemeral, pleasures. As Ovid wittily shows us, there is no eroticism in the definitive possession of something that can be neither won nor lost. Narcissus's encounter with himself is fundamentally non-erotic, in that his desire is always already fulfilled; yet also, paradoxically, overwhelmingly so, in that it can never be fulfilled in the way that he wants it to be.

'Iste ego sum'

We are told that Narcissus's death comes about as a result of knowing himself, and this self-knowledge is erotic: knowledge of himself as both subject and object of desire. In Ovid's account, this experience is meant to avenge Narcissus's many spurned lovers, one of whom finally prays in frustration: 'sic amet ipse licet, sic non potiatur amato!' [So may he himself love, and not gain the thing he loves] (*Met.* III, 405). One might imagine that the experience would give Narcissus some insight into the pain he has caused others by his resistance to love. Again, from a medieval perspective, true self-knowledge would include a penitential recognition of arrogant self-absorption, as well as a passage beyond all worldly love, as the soul's desire is fixed on God.[7] Narcissus's avenger makes no such request, however; and Narcissus learns no such thing. As far as one can tell from Ovid's text, all that he gleans from his ordeal is precisely what his spurned would-be lover requested: the immediate, and largely ineffable, knowledge of impossible desire. And that lesson has already been learnt long before the dramatic moment of self-recognition. From his first glance into the watery mirror, he knows himself as an object of desire, as well as knowing what it is to desire, and he reads the effects of this desire on his own face.[8] In moral terms, it is this utter abandonment to eros that prevents him — like the Lover in the *Rose* — from putting his new self-knowledge to any constructive use.

Even after his moment of insight, Narcissus continues to address his image as 'puer' [boy]. He blames the image for its disappearance when his tears, rippling the water, cause it to break up: 'quo refugis? remane nec me, crudelis, amantem / desere!' [Oh, whither do you flee? Stay here, and desert not him who loves thee, cruel one] (*Met.* III, 477–78). As Ovid tells the story, then, that fateful moment — 'iste ego sum' [I am he] (463) — brings no moral enlightenment, but only despair. The deceptive and destructive qualities of erotic knowledge, and the dangers thereby posed, are an important motif in the use of Narcissus by medieval French poets.

When Guillaume de Lorris's Lover looks into the fountain he, too, acquires a searing knowledge of desire and of himself as desiring subject; and he recognizes this knowledge as simultaneously revelation and deception. On the one hand, the crystals offer a comprehensive vision:

> tot autresi vos di por voir
> que li cristaus sanz decevoir
> tot l'estre dou vergier encuse
> a celui qui en l'eve muse. (*RR*, 1557–60)

> [similarly I tell you truly that the crystal, without deception, reveals the entire being of the orchard to one who stares into the water.]

Yet the Lover also comments ruefully that 'Cil miroërs m'a deceü' [this mirror deceived me] (*RR*, 1607). The mirror not only reveals a detailed allegory of desire, but also instils that desire in the beholder. The deceiving knowledge that it offers is of a painful lack, one whose fulfilment — equally illusory — will be subject to the whims of Fortune. In that sense, the erotic self-knowledge that killed Narcissus, and now afflicts the Lover, is actually self-deception. Indeed, this very point is made by Genius when, some nineteen thousand lines later, he condemns the Fountain of Narcissus for its inability to offer any kind of clear vision to those who attempt to see themselves in its waters: 'Tuit s'i forsanent et s'angoissent / por ce que point ne s'i connoissent' [they all lapse into madness and anguish there, because they don't recognize themselves at all] (*RR*, 20407–08).[9]

'A nostro secedere corpore'

In Chapter 1 I described the onset of desire as a splitting of the poetic self. Cupid's interventions in both the *Amores* and the *Rose* create a doubling of the poetic voice, now split between an authorial persona and an even more fictional protagonist. And the amorous persona himself must take on further duplicity if he is to succeed in the erotic quest. It is therefore of interest to note that the first wish expressed by Narcissus after his flash of recognition, is for a separation from himself:

> O utinam a nostro secedere corpore possem!
> Votum in amante novum, vellem, quod amamus, abesset. (*Met.* III, 467–68)

> [Oh, that I might be parted from my own body! and, strange prayer for a lover, I would that what I love were absent from me!]

Most immediately, of course, this reflects Narcissus's wish for an external object, an 'other' through whom to route his desire. Having come to perceive himself both as lacking, and as possessing that which would fill the lack, he has short-circuited the normal operations of eros. Only if the object of desire is removed — 'vellem, quod amamus, abesset' — is it possible to experience the delightful fantasy of reunion.

But Narcissus's wish takes on an even more interesting aspect in the context of poetic and amorous duplicity. The trajectory of the *Rose* implies a need to detach from oneself as desiring subject, and to make that desire itself an object of knowledge. Once he understands the 'jeus d'Amors', the would-be lover is, in effect, split internally between the knowledgeable codifier and the actor; he can craft his persona, or indeed the innumerable different personae required by the different situations into which his love will lead him. The erotic quest will fail, however, if he is unable to achieve that distance from himself. As we have seen, this is a crucial distinction between Guillaume's *Rose* and the *Amores*, where Ovid can stand back, speak as poet, and ultimately take his leave of the project: 'inbelles elegi, genialis Musa, valete' [Unwarlike elegies, congenial Muse, O fare ye well] (*Am.* III.xv, 19). Ovid's *Amores* offer an analogy for the transformations undergone by Guillaume's persona. But Guillaume's Lover is a far cry from the sexually experienced, ironically self-conscious persona of the *Amores*; if anything, he illustrates the dangers of taking Ovid at his word. Like Narcissus, he sees the impossibility of his desire while yet believing in its illusions, and lacks the ability to exploit illusion as a strategy in the necessary deception of himself and others. It will be Jean de Meun who, as it were, restores the split in the poetic 'I'; once the inscribed author is no longer identified with the Lover, the first-person voice is literally separated from itself.[10]

In keeping with this ironic doubling of the narrative voice, the Lover learns to embrace duplicity. He welcomes the assistance of Faux Semblant, and adapts to what he had earlier, and more naïvely, resisted as 'deablie' [devilry] (*RR*, 7767). Having silenced Male Bouche, Faux Semblant indulges in a forty-three-line fantasy outlining the means of subterfuge and deception whereby 'du bouton s'apressast / li fins amanz' [the refined lover would capture the rosebud] (*RR*, 12498–99). The Lover instantly sees that this is the narrative he wishes to follow, no doubt finding it far preferable to the endless torments of desire that were prescribed some ten thousand lines earlier by the God of Love. And so he vows that he will act 'si con Faus Semblant ot pensé; / du tout m'en tign a son pensé' [just as Faux Semblant thought; may I hold completely to his plan] (*RR*, 12509–10). The advent of Faux Semblant allows the Lover finally to take on a self-consciously fictional aspect. His desire for the Rose, a poetic construct in itself, has now become the hidden truth lying beneath a fictional façade constructed and manipulated by the Lover. By the end of the poem, with his pilgrim staff and his pouch of hammers, the Lover has been allegorized into a figure of male sexuality. As such he can finally access the equally allegorical love object, while the narrator comments, both lewdly and sententiously, on their ecstatic union.

The trope of separating from oneself is repeated in another Ovidian myth, that of Marsyas. Marsyas was seen as relevant to the *Rose* by at least one early reader, the author of a late-thirteenth-century interpolation found in at least twenty manuscripts, in which Cupid tells the story of Marsyas during his midpoint rallying of the troops.[11] Love plays no part in the demise of the hapless satyr, who is flayed alive in punishment for having challenged Apollo with his rustic flute. But his dying lament in Ovid's account is noteworthy:

> 'quid me mihi detrahis?' inquit;
> 'a! piget, a! non est' clamabat 'tibia tanti.' (*Met.* VI, 385–86)

['Why do you tear me from myself?' he cried. 'Oh, I repent! Oh, a flute is not worth such a price!']

Though Ovid alludes only briefly to this tale in the *Metamorphoses*, he elaborates on the flute's associations with Athena in the *Ars amatoria*, in warning women against displays of anger:

> Pertinet ad faciem rabidos compescere mores:
> [...]
> Ora tument ira: migrescunt sanguine venae:
>   Lumina Gorgoneo saevius igne micant.
> 'I procul hinc,' dixit 'non es mihi, tibia, tanti,'
>   Ut vidit vultus Pallas in amne suos.
> Vos quoque si media speculum spectetis in ira,
>   Cognoscat faciem vix satis ulla suam. (*Ars* III, 501, 503–08)

[it is beauty's task to hold mad moods in check [...] The face becomes swollen with passion; the veins grow black with blood, the eyes flash more savagely than Gorgon fire. 'Away with you,' said Pallas, 'to me, flute, you are not worth the cost,' when she saw her countenance in the stream. And you, should you in mid-passion behold a mirror, scarce one of you would know her own features.]

The flute, then, is associated with a disfigurement inappropriate to wisdom and to eros alike, one that exposes a shameful interior, normally hidden, to public view. Marsyas's comment on the 'price' of the flute echoes that of Athena almost verbatim. And the gruesome account of his flaying repeats the reference to the swollen veins of the raging woman, as the victim's breast is laid bare for all to see:

> [...] trepidaeque sine ulla
> pelle micant venae; salientia viscera possis
> et perlucentes numerare in pectore fibras. (*Met.* VI, 389–91)

[his veins throb and quiver with no skin to cover them: you could count the entrails as they palpitate, and the vitals showing clearly in his breast.]

If Narcissus suffered from an inability to separate from himself, Marsyas undergoes that process literally, as bodily dismemberment.

What has the tale of Marsyas to do with the *Rose*? A brief consideration of the Marsyas interpolation and its relationship to the surrounding text will help to clarify certain themes of the poem that must have led to its insertion by an early reader. Asserting his enmity with 'Juno la vieille' [the old woman Juno], Cupid explains that his feelings for his aunt are similar to those of Apollo for Marsyas, and proceeds to summarize the story with elements drawn from both the *Ars* and the *Metamorphoses*:

> Chier compera sa fole verve,
> Mar vit la buisine Minerve,

> Qu'el jeta dedenz la palu.
> De buisiner ne li chalu,
> Pour ce que li dieu se rioient
> De ses joues qui li enfloient
> Quant el buisinoit a leur table.
> Le satyreau tieng a coupable.
> [...]
> A l'arbre pendu l'escorcha
> Phebus tout vif; tant le torcha
> Par tout une seule plaie ot,
> De par tout li sans li raiot,
> Et criot: 'Las! pour quoi l'empris?
> N'iert pas buisine en si grant pris!'
> (ed. Langlois, vv. 21–28, 35–40)

[He paid dearly for his foolish bravado, woe that he saw Minerva's flute, which she threw into the marsh. She didn't want to play it, because the gods made fun of how her cheeks puffed out when she played the flute at their table. I blame the satyr. [...] Phebus flayed him alive, hung from a tree; he scraped at him so much that he was a single wound all over, blood ran from everywhere, and he cried: 'Alas! Why did I do it? A flute is not worth such a great price!']¹²

In Cupid's retelling, Marsyas's performance is explicitly juxtaposed with the disfigurement eschewed by Athena. And intriguingly, he is analogous to Juno, scorned by Cupid as 'la vieille' — hardly an innocent term in the context of the *Rose*, where a figure identified by that very term is about to emerge in all her hideous glory. Though la Vieille does enable to Lover to have a meeting with Bel Acueil, her ethos of feminine self-interest and the commodification of sex runs counter to the interests of the male Lover, and he contemptuously dismisses her as a 'fausse vieille et serve' [false, low-class old woman] (*RR*, 12958). In the *Metamorphoses*, Juno is also the sworn enemy of love, or more properly of male erotic desire, as she works tirelessly to thwart the amorous trysts of her husband and to punish his lovers. Small wonder that this ever-jealous goddess is targeted by Cupid as a particularly odious enemy.

Though Cupid's reasoning in the *Rose* interpolation remains somewhat obscure, we can see at least that he sets up an analogy between Juno — the vengeful persecutor of love — and Marsyas, who 'contre Phebus buisinot' [played the flute in a contest against Phebus] (ed. Langlois, v. 30). The implied association of Cupid with Apollo might be unexpected, but should not really surprise. Apollo, after all, is a frequently amorous god himself; and as we saw above, it is Apollo who authorizes the Ovidian application of Delphic self-knowledge to the careful crafting of erotic allure. In an Ovidian context, Apollo is the bridge between wisdom and erotic duplicity — a bridge that is most appropriately made, we must agree, by the god of poetry. Marsyas's rustic piping and his crude antics might have their place, but they cannot compete with the self-crafting and self-transcendence of a poetry born of the cooperation between Cupid and Apollo. Indeed, the bodily, lusty music produced by Marsyas might even be seen as a burlesque parody of Apollonian harmonies. The love that Apollo and Cupid foster is cultivated through a careful and highly selective oscillation between concealment and revelation of the fears and desires of both lover and beloved. Poetry in the tradition retrospectively defined by the *Rose* — a tradition both erotic and philosophical — does allow for a revelation of inner feelings and erotic secrets, but always in fictional and figural form, not in the literal manner of a Marsyas.

Cupid's association of Marsyas with Juno has further implications for the *Rose*. Bearing in mind Juno's association with jealousy, and her ruthless exposure and punishment of any girl unfortunate enough to attract Jove's interest, we might read the interpolated lines as implying an identification of Marsyas with Male Bouche. And in this sense, his crime — 'contre Phebus buisinot' — could be understood not only in the specific sense of challenging Apollo to a musical contest, but also in a more general sense of publicly defaming him, or debasing the musical arts with which Apollo is associated. As his name implies, Male Bouche is the personification of speech — specifically, of a prurient discourse that seeks constantly to defame and thwart the followers of Cupid. Whereas Cupid is committed to euphemistic speech and decorous behaviour — albeit as a screen for the furtherance of bodily drives best left unmentioned — Male Bouche's role is to articulate the sordid underside of that courtly exterior.[13] In keeping with this role, Guillaume de Lorris portrays Male Bouche as playing a variety of rustic wind instruments — including *buisines* — as he broadcasts his 'poetic' discourse of love unmasked and revealed as wanton lechery:

> Il monte le soir as quarniaus
> et atrempre ses chalumiaus
> et ses buisines et ses cors;
> une foiz dit chanz et descors
> et sons noviaus de controvaille
> as estives de Cornuaille,
> autre foiz dit a la flaüte
> c'onques ne trova fame jute:
> 'Il n'est nule qui ne se rie
> c'ele ot parler de lecherie;
> ceste est pute, ceste se farde,
> et ceste folement regarde.' (*RR*, 3877–88)

[In the evening he climbs up to the battlements and tunes his flutes and his pipes and horns; sometimes he sings songs and 'discords' and newly crafted tunes on Cornish pipes; other times he sings, along with the flute, that he never found a faithful woman: 'There is no woman who does not laugh if she hears tell of lechery; this one is a whore, that one paints her face, and that one looks about lustfully.']

In considering Male Bouche's relevance to the Marsyas story, we can almost see him as analogous to the flute itself: a perniciously crafted voice, a means of revealing that which might better be concealed.

If Marsyas is inserted into the *Rose* as a figure for Male Bouche, his demise — the exposure of a distasteful interior — prepares for the scene some 1500 lines later in which Faux Semblant induces Male Bouche to make his confession, then uses that moment of submission as an opportunity to strangle the troublesome tattler and cut out his tongue. Turning his talent for slander onto himself, Male Bouche for the first time reveals his own failings, and thereby the hypocrisy of his moralizing tale-telling. Confessional self-revelation robs the moralist of his authority; he is suddenly split, becoming both the subject and the object of discourse. It is this precarious balancing act — the simultaneous construction and dissolution of the self — that must be managed both by the love poet, and by the Lover with his myriad roles and guises.

The poetic project of the *Rose* promises to take the Lover outside himself in a positive sense, in a union with the other. And it promises to take the reader beyond him or herself as well, offering new knowledge, new ways of experiencing desire. A sense of revelation and novelty, touching and being touched by the 'other', is essential to both bodily and textual erotics. But is this 'newness' really to be trusted, or is it yet another facet of the duplicitous discourse of love?[14] Is the desiring subject forever trapped between the stagnant self-containment of Narcissus, and the traumatic violation of boundaries experienced by Marsyas? To consider these questions, we must return to the beginning of the poem, and re-examine the Lover's initiation into love.

'Et quomodo iam inveniam te, si memor non sum tui?'

In thinking that the garden is real and that he can be a player in it, as we saw in Chapter 1, the Lover misreads its allegorical nature. As a poetic image, it can never be an object of either desire or knowledge in itself, but only a medium through which to access knowledge of a different order. His love object, the Rose, is particularly enigmatic. Rather than falling in love with one of the personified inhabitants of the garden, his choice falls on part of the garden itself. Perhaps the garden and its inhabitants cannot really be distinguished; they make up a single allegorical construct. As object of erotic desire, the Rose highlights the extent to which the Lover, rather like Narcissus, mistakes fictions for realities.

Even once we recognize that the Rose is more symbolic than real, the indeterminacy of its meaning casts a veil over the Lover's experience. It has often been pointed out that the initial description of the 'bouton' on its stiff, straight stem implies an image far more phallic than feminine.[15] If we accept it as a phallic symbol, the Lover's fascination with the *bouton* might indicate that he, like Narcissus, is discovering his own sexuality. His immediate impulse is to reach out and grasp the Rose — something Cupid's volley of arrows prevents him from accomplishing, for he is struck down every time he tries to make a move. As a figure of desire, after all, Cupid has no interest in allowing the amorous quest to be completed quite that easily. The Lover must learn to see the Rose as something inaccessible; even more importantly, his desire must conform to the poetic and amorous codes that now define his being. The arrows that enter the Lover's eye to lodge in his heart might seem to represent the qualities that aroused his desire: Biauté, Simpleice, Cortoisie, Compaignie and Biau Samblant [Beauty, Simplicity, Courtesy, Company and Fair Semblance]. Yet the Lover already felt the full force of desire before seeing the Rose, as is clear from the narrative sequence:

> Quant cele rage m'ot si pris,
> dont maint autre ont esté sorpris,
> vers les rosiers tantost me trés;

> [...]
> Icil bouton mout m'enbelurent,
> onques si bel nu leu ne crurent.
> [...]
> Entre les autres en eslui
> un si tres bel [...]
>   (*RR*, 1621–23, 1647–48, 1653–54)

[When this frenzy had gripped me, which has ambushed many others, I immediately headed towards the rose bushes [...] Those buds greatly delighted me; never did such beautiful ones grow anywhere else [...] Amongst the others, I selected one very beautiful one.]

Cupid waits until his victim has selected an object of desire before firing his arrows:

> et quant il ot aperceü
> que j'avoie ensint esleü
> ce bouton, qui plus me seoit
> que nul des autres ne fessoit,
> il a tantost pris une floiche. (*RR*, 1683–87)

[and when he saw that I had chosen that bud, which pleased me more than any other flower did, at once he took an arrow.]

As each arrow strikes him, the Lover attempts to pull it out, but is invariably unsuccessful. The first, Biauté, 'm'ot si dedenz le cuer fichiee / qu'ele n'en pot estre esrachiee, / ançois remest encore dedens' [so lodged in my heart that it could not be taken out, and it still remains there] (*RR*, 1715–17); and it is the same with all the others. The arrows serve not to create desire but to intensify it by shaping and prolonging it, as they are incorporated into the Lover's heart.[16]

The arrows' dramatic impact on the Lover can be seen as the awakening of memory; for he has already noted all five of the arrows during the carol scene several hundred lines earlier (*RR*, 935–56). Two of them, Biauté and Cortoisie, additionally figured in personified form among the carollers themselves (*RR*, 992–1016, 777–85, 1227–42). And both made a particular impression on the Lover during his fleeting participation in the carol. Biauté occasions a memory of his earlier glimpse of this quality in the form of an arrow: 'cele dame avoit non Biautez, / ausi come une des .v. floiches' [this lady was named Beauty, like one of the arrows] (*RR*, 992–93). And in describing Biauté, he stresses the extent to which this ideal is housed in his memory, exerting its magic on his heart:

> mout grant douçour au cuer me touche,
> si m'aït Dex, quant il me menbre
> de la façon de chascune menbre,
> qu'il n'ot si bele fame ou monde. (*RR*, 1010–13)

[a great sweetness touches my heart, so help me God, when I remember the appearance of each part of her body, for there is no such beautiful woman in the world.]

As for Cortoisie, by the time we get to her description she too has already entered into the Lover's — and therefore the reader's — memory:

> C'est cele qui a la querole,
> la seue merci, m'apela
> tot maintenant que je vin la. (*RR*, 1230–32)

[She's the one who, thanks be to her, called me to the carol, as soon as I got there.]

When Biauté and Cortoisie later enter the Lover's heart in the form of arrows, we might see this as the memory of a memory.

But then, the love object itself is hardly a novel image. Roses first come to the Lover's attention in his encounter with Oiseuse, who wears them in her hair (*RR*, 553), as do Deduit and Cupid (*RR*, 827–28, 893–96). More importantly, roses serve as a standard of beauty. Deduit's companion, Leesce, 'resembloit rose novele' [resembled a newly-blooming rose]; of Biautez we are told that 'Tendre ot la char conme rose' [her flesh was as tender as a rose] (*RR*, 838, 999). Contemplation of the Rose — the absolute of feminine beauty — excites the Lover into a heightened awareness of an idealized feminine eroticism that crystallizes within him, even as he imagines himself to be discovering something new. In this sense too, he is like Narcissus (and Boethius), wishing to attain the Good by finding it outside himself, when it is actually lodged in his heart.

The Rose might also be an object of readerly desire, in that we are encouraged to look forward to a scene of consummation. More explicitly, however, the Rose is an object of endlessly deferred knowledge, as we ask ourselves what it is, or what it means. Guillaume's narrator promises to explain all that, saying that we will understand the dream once he has expounded it; but he never does. Our understanding of the Rose is as chimerical as is the Lover's enjoyment. The narrator strongly implies that he is leading us towards something hitherto unknown. As early as the prologue, he assures his readers that 'La matire est et bone et nueve' [the material is both good and new] (*RR*, 39), and he repeats this claim when he tantalizes the reader with promises of the dream's beautiful conclusion, stating that 'la matire en est novele' [its subject matter is new] (*RR*, 2064). But if Narcissus is the central model in Guillaume's text — and if Ovid and Boethius are formative figures for the tradition in which it is inscribed — perhaps we should seek that knowledge within ourselves. Ovid, after all, claimed that the ideal reader of the *Amores* would have experiential knowledge of love: desire must already have been felt before it can be either stoked or soothed. And it is probably impossible, in any case, to decode an allegory without already knowing the concepts that are represented in its figures.

But then, does any text ever really impart knowledge that the reader does not, in some sense, already have? Boethius gives prominent place to the notion that all learning is merely a remembering:

> Quisquis profunda mente vestigat verum
> Cupitque nullis ille deviis falli,
> In se revolvat intimi lucem visus
> Longosque in orbem cogat inflectens motus
> Animumque doceat quidquid extra molitur
> Suis retrusum possidere thesauris.
> [...]

Quod si Platonis musa personat verum,
Quod quisque discit immemor recordatur. (*CP* III, m. 11)

[Whoever with deep thought seeks out the truth / And wants not to go wrong
down devious ways, / Must on himself turn back the light of his inward vision, /
Bending and forcing his far-reaching movements / Into a circle, and must
teach his mind, / Whatever she is striving for without, / Removed within her
treasury to grasp. / [...] / If Plato's muse rings true, / What each man learns,
forgetful he recalls.]

According to the doctrine expounded here, we can encounter new and hitherto
unimagined fictions in poetry, but whatever knowledge or truth they contain will
already be within us, imprinted on our soul. The striking poetic image is a means
of awakening a dormant memory and of affording access to knowledge that has
slipped from consciousness, but it is not a source of new, hitherto non-existent
knowledge. We find the same concept in the theological context of Augustine's
Confessions.[17] Discussing his spiritual longing for God, and the long search that he
engaged in, he notes that it would be impossible for the soul to recognize God if it
did not have, imprinted within it, some memory of its Creator:

si praetor memoriam meam te invenio, immemor tui sum. et quomodo iam
inveniam te, si memor non sum tui? (*Conf.* 10.17, p. 122)

[If I now find thee not by my memory, then am I unmindful of thee: and how
shall I find thee if I do not remember thee?]

The idea would certainly have been familiar to any medieval writer with the literary knowledge manifested by Guillaume de Lorris. What is intriguing is the way
that he explores its relevance not to intellectual or spiritual illumination, but to
erotic love.[18]

For the Lover, the Rose represents his aspirations to a courtly ideal, created and
defined through poetry, but experienced by him as real in an absolute sense; a vision
born from his internalization of symbolic constructs, but experienced as something
entirely new. Central to this ideal is desire: a mimetic desire shaped by the society
around him, but experienced by the Lover, once again, as personal to him, inspired
by the sight of an object that — despite being one of countless rosebuds in the
garden — is unique in its capacity to heal his wounds. This desire was visited upon
the resisting Narcissus in an extreme form, causing him to love not just the same
ideals, but the exact same incarnation of those ideals, as those he had scorned:
namely, himself. Its fulfilment, never absolute but only ever partial and fleeting,
depends upon an enduring belief in the difference of the self from the object of
desire, and also on a split within the self that allows desire to be staged without the
self being lost. The experience entails a particular kind of self-knowledge, whereby
the self can be crafted as a perfect embodiment of the erotic ideal. And it also
depends on self-deception, in its avoidance of the knowledge that this ideal can
never be real, but only imperfectly staged, an imitation of a fictional model. It is
the former — knowledge of the eroticized self — that is parodied in the disastrous
self-knowledge of Narcissus. And within the context of the *Rose*, the punishment
meted out to Marsyas — exposure of a throbbing, overflowing interior antithetical
to either love or wisdom — is a parodic unmasking of the duplicity inherent in

the crafting of both the erotic and the poetic self. Associating Marsyas with the counter-discourse of the *mesdisants* and *losengiers* — like Guillaume's association of Narcissan self-delusion with the resistant enemies of love — is part of the very process of duplicity that permits erotic discourse to present itself as truthful and self-abasing.

For the male reader — for it is male desire, despite the prologue dedication, that the poem addresses — the Rose and the arrows triggered by its contemplation might also elicit a mimetic desire and an aspiration to the courtly ideals propounded in the poem. This construction, in other words, aims to inspire an erotic awakening, telling the receptive reader which qualities will define his desire just as soon as he finds an object on which to focus it. But as a literary figure, it is also central to an erotics of reading, and in that sense we might identify the Rose with the illusion that we can actually acquire new knowledge from poetry, and that there can be any true knowledge of the 'other' that is separate from self-knowledge. If eroticism lies in the deferral of jouissance, still it depends on a belief that jouissance exists and is the ultimate goal, however long it may take to attain it. And the belief that we will receive some kind of illumination, some insight or knowledge of something new, motivates us to keep reading the poetic text.[19] If ever it became clear that we had that knowledge already, there would no longer be any sense of deferral. Rather than taking us outside ourselves, the text would only be taking us back into ourselves; and within the framework of erotic desire, there might seem little point in reading it at all. If we had no concept of an endpoint to the trajectory, we might also be inclined to abandon the project, having lost the pleasure of anticipation. The prolongation of readerly desire depends on this fiction of the 'other', something that must be known through glimpses that provide an inkling of its rewards, while also remaining unknown so that its eventual unveiling provides the excitement of the new. The reader's pleasure, in turn, lies in the allure of the poetic fictions — exotic, shocking, splendid — that keep this promised knowledge at the very edges of our view.

'Scripta [...] non in tabulis lapideis, sed in tabulis cordis carnalibus'

In the Christian mythographic and exegetical tradition that would have been well known to an educated poet like Jean de Meun, the motif of a longed-for unmediated encounter brings to mind Paul's famous discussion of the soul's knowledge of God, in which he contrasts the highly mediated knowledge accessible in earthly life with the clarity of vision that is possible only in death:

> Videmus nunc per speculum in aenigmate: tunc autem facie ad faciem. Nunc cognosco ex parte: tunc autem cognoscam sicut et cognitus sum. (1 Corinthians 13. 12)

> [For now we see through a glass, darkly; but then face to face: now I know in part; but then I shall know even as also I am known.][20]

Though the soul may long for absolute knowledge of God, while still imprisoned in the flesh it is incapable of experiencing it. We require the mediation of a mirror — a visual and symbolic code of images, language and dogma — in order to approach the mystery of divinity. Techniques of exegesis enable us to access hidden meanings; but even these are still expressed symbolically, and articulated by means of human language. A closer approach to divine revelation may be made by turning inward, but even this contemplative approach cannot escape the need for a kind of reading or decoding. The image of God imprinted in the human soul is, itself, an internalized 'text':

> Hoc autem testamentum quod testabor ad illos post dies illos dicit Dominus: dando leges meas in cordibus eorum et in mente eorum superscribam eas. (Hebrews 10. 16)

> [This is the covenant that I will make with them after those days, saith the Lord, I will put my laws into their hearts, and in their minds will I write them.]

In the public realm, humans can know one another only through the medium of symbolically constructed identities, the outward manifestation of the divine 'epistle' written in the human heart:

> Epistola nostra vos estis, scripta in cordibus nostris, quae scitur, et legitur ab omnibus hominibus: manifestati quod epistula estis Christi, ministrata a nobis, scripta non atramento, sed Spiritu Dei vivi: non in tabulis lapideis, sed in tabulis cordis carnalibus. (II Corinthians 3. 2–3)

> [Ye are our epistle, written in our hearts, known and read of all men: forasmuch as ye are manifestly declared to be the epistle of Christ ministered by us, written not with ink, but with the Spirit of the living God; not in tables of stone, but in fleshly tables of the heart.]

When Paul looks forward to knowing God 'even as also I am known', he does not mean that he will know God as he is known by other people or even as he knows himself; but that he will know God in the immediacy and clarity with which he is now known by God, and by God alone.

As our reading of the *Rose* has suggested, the knowledge of God as defined in these familiar passages is analogous to the equally impossible desire for, and fear of, unmediated sexual knowledge. The *Rose* could be seen as illustrating — perhaps even as delighting in — an idea similar to Lacan's famous statement that 'there is no sexual relationship', for the sexual other can never truly be known 'face to face'.[21] Sexual knowledge, like the knowledge of God, can be glimpsed only by means of symbolic constructs, 'through a glass darkly'. The *Rose* explores the dynamics of erotic desire, in part, as a parody of spiritual desire; and this parodic spirit reaches a particularly audacious climax in the discourse of Genius.[22]

In his sermon to Love's barons, Genius outlines a critique of Guillaume's Garden of Delight, with particular attention to the images on the outer wall, the carol, and the fountain of Narcissus.[23] This construct is then compared, unfavourably, to the 'Biaus Parc' of Heaven, in which a Good Shepherd watches over his flock of sheep in a beautiful meadow that is graced by a three-streamed (yet also single-streamed) fountain containing a tri-faceted (yet spherical) carbuncle, and an olive tree. Genius thus creates a model that moves from the perilous fountain and inaccessible Rose of erotic desire, to the salvific fountain of the Trinity and the olive with its 'fruit de salu' [fruit of salvation] (*RR*, 20493). Genius's gloss parodies the Pauline movement

outlined in I Corinthians 13 from a vision 'per speculum in aenigmate' towards
one that is 'facie ad faciem', as well as that outlined in II Corinthians 3 from the
obfuscations of the 'old law' to the revelations of the New Testament.[24] The vision
afforded by the fountain that 'tua le biau Narcisus' [killed the fair Narcissus] (RR,
20380) is actually one of blindness: 'chascuns qui sa teste i boute / por soi mirer, il
n'i voit goute' [anyone who sticks his head in there to see [himself], sees nothing at
all] (RR, 20405–06). The Heavenly Park, in contrast, offers an illuminating vision
of the Trinitarian Godhead, albeit that we here below can conceive of it only in the
metaphorical form — per speculum in aenigmate — of a logic-defying fountain that
'sourt de soi-meïsmes' [arises from itself] (RR, 20450) containing a geometrically
impossible carbuncle. Rather than a bewitching play of colours, the Trinitarian
fountain is characterized by a pure radiance that illuminates the park and enlightens
the minds of those who behold it. The detailed contrast that Genius elaborates
between the Garden and the Park, associating the former with death, blindness and
obfuscation and the latter with life, enlightenment and revelation, is itself a skewed
reflection of the Pauline contrast in II Corinthians 3 between Jew and Christian:
'sed obtusi sunt sensus eorum. Usque in hodiernum enim diem, idipsum velamen
in lectione veteris testamenti manet non revelatum (quoniam in Christo evacuator)'
[But their minds were blinded: for unto this day remaineth the same veil untaken
away in the reading of the old testament; which veil is done away in Christ]
(II Corinthians 3. 14). Just as Paul notes that God 'idoneos nos fecit ministros novi
testamenti' [hath made us able ministers of the New Testament] (II Corinthians
3. 6), Genius calls for his audience to go forth and preach Nature's law: 'ma dame
en sa lai / a mestier de preescheeurs' [my lady needs preachers for her law] (RR,
19896–97). And Genius's final summation of the two constructs — 'cele les vis de
mort anivre, / mes ceste fet les morz revivre' [that one intoxicates the living with
death, but this one brings the dead back to life] (RR, 20595–96) — recalls one of
Paul's most famous lines: 'littera enim occidit, Spiritus autem vivificat' [for the
letter killeth, but the spirit giveth life] (II Corinthians 3. 6).

　　Genius's own obfuscation, however, turns on the interpretation of just what sort
of heavenly bliss and immortality are really on offer in the Park.[25] While it is easy to
imagine that the contrast pits material and erotic desire against spiritual fulfilment,
the full text of Genius's sermon invites a different reading, one that opposes the
courtly flirtation and protraction of desire in Deduit's garden to the prospect of
sexual fulfilment and procreative 'immortality' represented in the Park. Indeed, the
moral advice that Genius offers at the end of his sermon is borrowed from Ovid's Ars
(I, 640–42).[26] These admonitions to avoid fraud, theft and murder — and to engage
in Nature's work — are presented as the distilled essence of Genius's teaching: 'je
vos reveill briefmant retrere / tretout quan que vos devez fere' [I want to briefly
sum up everything you need to do] (RR, 20605–06). But the original context of
these precepts is Ovid's exhortation to deceive women freely: 'Nec timide promitte:
trahunt promissa puellas / [...] / Ludite, si sapitis, solas impune puellas' (Ars I, 631,
643) [Nor be timid in your promises; by promises women are betrayed [...] If you are
wise, cheat women only, and avoid trouble]. The passage continues with the advice
that men should achieve sexual satisfaction by whatever means necessary: 'Exemplo

doleat femina laesa suo / [...] / Vim licet appelles: grata est vis ista puellis' (*Ars* I, 658, 673) [let the woman feel the smart of a wound she first inflicted [...] You may use force; women like you to use it]. Despite his appropriation of Scriptural imagery, Genius's only real concern is to promote heterosexual consummation at all cost.

In the first half of his sermon Genius, like his model in Alain de Lille's *De planctu naturae*, proclaims his condemnation of sodomites; going somewhat further, however, Jean's Genius also speaks out against castration and even celibacy.[27] Somewhat surprisingly — one could think of more obvious examples — the figure he chooses as the representative of his ideal is Cadmus. Despite the fact that the resulting 'progeny' immediately set to killing one another, Cadmus's sowing of the dragon's teeth is glossed as procreation. Genius's reading results from what we might call an allegoresis of the second degree: it was standard in medieval mythographic tradition to gloss Cadmus's adventure as an allegory for the invention of writing, and of course for Genius writing itself is but an allegory for begetting.[28] Genius does, perhaps, eliminate the erotic tension that pervades Guillaume's *vergier*, but only to replace it with a focus on active sexuality. Rather than allegorizing sexual content into spiritual dogma or mystical transport, in other words, Genius identifies procreative sexuality itself as the means to salvation and life everlasting. Even more audaciously, he plays on the sexual connotations of the 'fleshy tables' of II Corinthians 3.3. The motif of procreative 'writing' is adapted from Alain de Lille, but the effects of this allegorical redeployment are more striking in the pseudo-theological context of Jean's Genius, with its confusion of the sexual and the spiritual. In Paul's formulation, all of humanity is subsumed into a feminine subject-position with regard to the masculine God, who writes 'in tabulis cordis carnalibus'. The divine image, impressed into each of us in the form of an ethical conscience, allows us to access, albeit dimly, some understanding of God. Medieval devotional texts frequently employ the motif of reading metaphorical books within the mind, variously identified with the self-scrutiny of the conscience, the act of meditating on the life of Christ, or a contemplative discovery of the insights afforded by divine Grace.[29]

In the procreative model of the *Rose*, however, humanity is divided along gendered lines, with the attribution of 'greffes' and 'tables' respectively identifying male and female. Male 'writing' impresses the form of the man's likeness onto the 'table' of the female body, producing an heir in the image of the father. Genius does complain that the followers of Orpheus — those who misuse their sexual anatomy in a failure to procreate — misread the law of Nature, noting that 'a rebours ses regles lisent' [they read her rules against the grain] (*RR*, 19628). This misreading, however, is also an improper writing, a corruption of the great 'text' that is the natural world with its endless generations: 'ainz pervertissent l'escriture / quant il vienent a la lecture' [thus they pervert the writing when they come to read it] (*RR*, 19631–32). In the sexual context established by Genius, the most crucial directive is no longer to read within one's own heart, but to write on the body of the sexual other: 'greffes avez, pansez d'escrire' [you have styluses, remember to write] (*RR*, 19764). Though it is not articulated as such, the cumulative effect of his sermon is to imply a shocking de-sublimation: the finger of God, writing in the fleshy tables of the heart, has become the penis writing on the tables of the vulva. This scandalous (if merely implicit) conflation of Alain de Lille's procreative 'writing' with the spiritual writing of God no doubt contributes to Jean Gerson's fury at the discourse of Genius. Here, he states, Jean de Meun 'n'eust mie pis fait de getter le teuxte des Euvangilles ou l'imaige du cruxefis en une grant fange orde et parfonde' [would not have behaved any worse in throwing the Gospels or the image of the Crucifixion into a deep and filthy pit of mud].[30] Noting that much of the passage is 'corrumpuement estraitte du grant Alain' [extracted in corrupted form from the great Alain], he points out that the latter author 'ne parla onques en tele maniere' [never spoke in such a manner].[31] But of course it was never Jean's intent merely to produce a compilation of wisdom from the Latin authors: the distortions to which he subjects their material, as I have argued, are the very means by which he generates the amorous and sexual knowledge so tantalizingly promised throughout the poem. The spiritual writing in the heart is the 'text' through which our closest approach to divinity is mediated. Similarly, according to Genius, the unknowable mysteries of the other's body, and of the 'rapport sexuel' itself, are mediated through the 'writing' of sexual intercourse. Both spiritual and erotic knowledge lie outside language; both can be approached through a variety of enigmas, both linguistic and visual; both are most closely expressed in a metaphoric writing, one of the heart, the other of the genitals.

'Toutes vos choses / sunt en vos meïsmes encloses'

At the conclusion of the *Rose*, as the Lover's path is cleared and the obstacles fall away, the poetic language becomes increasingly dense, with a profusion of allegorical threads providing different metaphors for sexual consummation. It is as though the fabric of the text itself is participating in the Lover's orgasm.[32] And while there can be no doubt that these closing lines depict, in some sense, an act of sexual intercourse, there is no explicit statement in the poem to that effect. Though the narrator advises the reader to pay close attention so that he, too, will know how to 'gather roses', no assistance is given in working out just how to put this advice into practice. For the reader, sexual jouissance is still very much *per speculum in aenigmate*. But then, in an erotics of reading, the final consummation must retain its allegorical veils if the reader's pleasure is to continue unabated. As Christine de Pizan noted, albeit unapprovingly, figurative language makes the *Rose*'s concluding passage 'six fois plus atisans et plus penetratis et plus delicteus a ceulx qui y sont enclins' [six times more stimulating and more penetrating and more delightful for those who are so inclined] than it would have been if the deed was openly stated; while Pierre Col cites with approval Jean's use of euphemistic terms such as 'jeu d'amours' [game of love] and 'tripot' [fooling around].[33] From a moralizing perspective, the danger of poetry lies in the eroticization of knowledge itself, as the reader delights more in the fictional screens of the fables than in the truths they are meant to transmit.

The philosophical and erotic axes along which the *Rose* unfolds define two different modes of seeing or of reading — one informed by a desire for knowledge to be recovered from its hiding-places in the mind, as a response to what one sees; the other informed by a desire for the object of the gaze itself, and the new, hitherto inaccessible experience that it promises to impart. The former seeks out objects that can trigger philosophical or spiritual awakening, while disavowing any interest in those objects themselves; the latter seeks out objects that awaken desire, while resisting the realization that this desire was always already present, primed to ignite as soon as the appointed target came into view. What I have termed the philosophical mode rests on the reassuring belief that one already has all that is needed for spiritual tranquillity and enlightenment; it imparts the sense of fulfilment expressed in the Old French *souffisance*, a quality praised by Reason in her efforts to re-educate the Lover. As she reminds him, 'toutes vos choses / sunt en vos meïsmes encloses' [all of your belongings are contained within yourself] (*RR*, 5311–12). The erotic mode imparts a painful sense of lack. But this is a delicious pain — a *dous mal* — because at the same time that it draws attention to a lack, it also identifies the marvellous object that will meet that lack in a wonderfully pleasurable way. In an erotic context, as Narcissus shows, nothing could be more of a let-down than to find oneself in a state of *souffisance*.

Within the fictions of the *Rose*, 'Guillaume de Lorris' — Jean's name for the Lover, whom he identifies as the poet of the first part — experiences the Rose as the promise of something new and exciting. The arrows of Love — winged words, flying straight to his heart to connect with memories of erotic allure — shape the inchoate 'noveile rage' [new passion] that he discovers at the fountain (*RR*, 1581). Cupid provides him with a poetic discourse that determines his experience of desire and renders it comprehensible. In Ovid's words, the Lover's initial *impetus* will become a more manageable *ratio*, albeit one that Reason herself will reject. In submitting himself to this symbolically determined order, the Lover has at least gratified his initial desire, which was quite simply to love — the 'd'amer volenté pure' [pure will to love] kindled at the fountain (*RR*, 1584). Thanks to the mediation of poetic language, that sudden, uncontrollable *rage* can now be experienced as *amors*. Yet for all that, he always professes surprise at each new turn of events, and his efforts to access the *bouton* serve only to place it definitively out of reach. We might almost wonder if the Lover really wants to reach the Rose at all. It is after all Bel Acueil for whom he most actively pines. The Rose is certainly the designated object of desire that provides the basis for the Lover's identity *qua* lover. But it is also a screen that keeps that desire obscure, and its means of fulfilment impossible clearly to imagine. In actual practice, the Lover's desire targets Bel Acueil: the atmosphere of receptivity that nurtures his fantasies about the Rose, but shows no sign of ever granting him possession. What the Lover wants is a means of periodically glimpsing the Rose, before he summons forth Dangier with a calculated transgression of Bel Acueil's very well-defined limits. Luxuriating in an indefinite suspension between *souvenir* and *esperance*, the Lover bides his time. No wonder Cupid despairs of ever seeing the poem completed.

It is Jean, imbued from birth with the full and comprehensive knowledge of amorous 'sciance', for whom the Rose will be a catalyst to intellectual remembrance, and a device for the presentation of this knowledge in poetic form.[34] I do not, of course, mean to impose this distinction on the historical authors themselves, though I would decidedly argue, against certain dissenting critical opinions, that the poem did have two authors.[35] Still less would I wish to imply that Jean's poem actually does reveal the totality of all possible knowledge about love and sexuality, or that whatever knowledge it imparts is in any way transparent.[36] But as they are presented within the poem, 'Guillaume de Lorriz' and 'Johans Chopinel' are the avatars for two fundamentally different, though complementary, approaches to the poetry of desire and erotic knowledge.

Notes to Chapter 2

1. For a summary of some of these views, with particular attention to the symbolism of the crystals in the fountain, see Larry H. Hillman, 'Another Look into the Mirror Perilous: The Role of the Crystals in the *Roman de la Rose*', *Romania*, 101 (1980), 225–38; Phillip McCaffrey, 'Guillaume de Lorris and Jean de Meun: Narcissus and Pygmalion', *Romanic Review*, 90 (1999), 435–49 (pp. 435–36).

2. Daniel Poirion argues that Narcissan dangers are overcome only in Jean's continuation, in 'Narcisse et Pygmalion dans le *Roman de la Rose*', in *Essays in Honor of Louis Francis Solano*, ed. by Raymond J. Cormier and Urban T. Holmes (Chapel Hill: University of North Carolina Press, 1970), pp. 153–65. Pascal Antonietti sees the dangers of phantasmagorical images and narcissistic self-absorption as a central theme of the poem, in '"C'est li mireors perilleus": Images et miroirs dans *Le Roman de la Rose*', in *Le Moyen Âge dans la modernité*, ed. by Jean R. Scheidegger, Sabine Girardet and Eric Hicks (Paris: Champion, 1996), pp. 33–47. Jane Gilbert notes that belief in his escape from Narcissan delusion only confirms the Lover's subjection to that very delusion, in '"I am not he": Narcissus and Ironic Performativity in Medieval French Literature', *Modern Language Review*, 100 (2005), 940–53. Akbari, *Seeing*, asserts that the Lover 'reenacts the experience of Narcissus' (p. 51). In a more favourable reading of the Lover, Kessler, 'Quête amoureuse', argues that the Narcissus passage, which she see as 'le point culminant du texte et la clef à l'œuvre entière' [the culminating moment of the text and the key to the entire work], is dominated by 'l'idée centrale de dépassement' [the central idea of *dépassement*] (pp. 133, 135). Similar readings are offered by Uitti, '"Cele... [qui] doit estre rose clamee'"; Eric M. Steinle, 'Versions of Authority in the *Roman de la Rose*: Remarks on the Use of Ovid's Metamorphoses by Guillaume de Lorris and Jean de Meun', *Mediaevalia*, 13 (1987), 189–206 (p. 189); Georgette Kamenetz, 'La Promenade d'Amant comme experience mystique', in *Études sur le 'Roman de la Rose' de Guillaume de Lorris*, ed. by Jean Dufournet (Paris: Champion, 1984), pp. 83–104 (pp. 94–95).

3. See Robert Gregory, 'Reading as Narcissism: *Le Roman de la Rose*', *SubStance*, 12:2 [39] (1983), 37–48. Rosanna Brusegan characterizes the 'discours de la fontaine' [the discourse of the fountain] as 'une théorie de la connaissance' [a theory of knowledge], in 'L'Énumération et les chiffres du *Roman de la Rose* au *Tesoretto*', *Littérature*, 130 (June 2003), 48–67 (p. 53).

4. Fleming terms the gloss 'preposterous' in 'Jean de Meun', p. 98. For Poirion, it is a 'contre-sens' which nonetheless stresses that the rules of Love apply to all ('Narcise et Pygmalion', p. 157). Ann Tukey Harrison argues that Guillaume's moral is appropriated from the *Lai de Narcisus*, in 'Echo and Her Medieval Sisters', *The Centennial Review*, 26 (1982), 324–40; while Sarah Kay notes that 'it neatly illustrates the imbrication of the courtly with the misogynistic', in 'Sexual Knowledge: The Once and Future Texts of the *Romance of the Rose*', in *Textuality and Sexuality: Reading Theories and Practices*, ed. by Judith Still and Michael Worton (Manchester: Manchester University Press, 1993), pp. 69–86 (p. 78). Renate Blumenfeld-Kosinski finds the moral 'surprising' but nonetheless appropriate to the courtly model, in *Reading Myth: Classical Mythology and Its Interpretations in Medieval French Literature* (Stanford, CA: Stanford University Press, 1997), pp. 57–58. For a detailed discussion of the Narcissus passage and its critical reception, with particular attention to the import of the gloss, see Hult, *Self-fulfilling Prophecies*, pp. 263–300.

5. This document is not arranged alphabetically, but I employ the term 'index' for the sake of simplicity. See my '"Finding-Aids" for the Study of Vernacular Poetry in the Fourteenth

Century: The Example of the *Roman de la Rose*', in *Lesevorgänge. Prozesse des Erkennens in mittelalterlichen Texten, Bildern und Handschriften. Freiburger Colloquium 2007*, ed. by Eckart Conrad Lutz, Martina Backes and Stefan Matter, Medienwandel — Medienwechsel — Medienwissen, 11 (Zurich: Chronos, forthcoming 2010).

6. The majority of *Rose* manuscripts include an explicit allusion to Echo at this point, as reflected in Lecoy's edition: 'si con tu meïsmes le prueves / par Echo, sanz querre autres prueves' [as you prove it yourself by means of Echo, needing no further proof] (*RR*, vv. 5807–08). Although Echo's name is missing from MS 3874, the indexer could have known other copies of the poem, and remembered the analogy between the Lover and Narcissus. On Reason's identification with Echo, see Blumenfeld-Kosinski, *Reading Myth*, p. 71.

7. The twelfth-century *Narcisus* does allow for Narcissus to realize his errors and repent. See *Lai de Narcisus*, in *Pyrame et Thisbé, Narcisse, Philomena: Trois Contes du XIIe siècle imités d'Ovide*, ed. and trans. by Emmanuèle Baumgartner (Paris: Gallimard, 2000), vv. 941–68. On this text, see Albert Gier, 'L'Amour, les monologues: Le *Lai de Narcisse*', in *Conjunctures: Medieval Studies in Honor of Douglas Kelly*, ed. by Keith Busby and Norris J. Lacy (Amsterdam and Atlanta, GA: Rodopi, 1994), pp. 129–37; Goldin, *Mirror*, pp. 22–52; Harrison, 'Echo'.

8. Goldin notes that Narcissus '"doubled" himself [...] into knowing subject and known object' (*Mirror*, p. 34).

9. On this point see Blumenfeld-Kosinski, *Reading Myth*, pp. 84–85.

10. See my *From Song to Book*, pp. 90–95.

11. See my '*Romance of the Rose*', pp. 134–36. The Marsyas interpolation is printed by Langlois in his edition of the *Rose*, as a note to vv. 10830–31. In Lecoy's edition, the passage would follow v. 10800.

12. The Old French word *buisine* can refer to an instrument similar to a bagpipe or even a trumpet; I have used the word 'flute' because that is the term normally applied to Athena's instrument — a rustic flute or pipe of some sort.

13. It should be noted that Male Bouche's claims about the Lover are not actually false. As Fleming points out: 'Far from having told "lies" about the Lover, Malebouche has obviously been spreading the truth' ('*Roman de la Rose*', p. 171).

14. With respect to the *Rose* and its promises, Gally asks provocatively: 'Mais y-a-t-il rien de moins nouveau que l'art d'aimer?' [But is there anything less new than the art of love?] (*Intelligence*, p. 37).

15. See Gaunt, 'Bel Acueil'; Guynn, '*Roman de la Rose*', pp. 52–53; Uitti, '"Cele... [qui] doit estre rose clamee"'.

16. On this passage see Jean-Charles Payen, 'L'Art d'aimer chez Guillaume de Lorris', in *Études sur le 'Roman de la Rose' de Guillaume de Lorris*, ed. by Jean Dufournet (Paris: Champion, 1984), pp. 105–44 (pp. 117–19); Hult, *Self-fulfilling Prophecies*, pp. 230–33.

17. On Augustine's influence on Boethius, including the Neoplatonic doctrine of anamnesis, see Crabbe, 'Literary Design', pp. 251–63. On the importance of Augustine for Jean's portion of the *Rose*, see Fleming, *Reason and the Lover*. Fleming also touches on Augustinian elements in Boethius (pp. 46–51). I cite Augustine, *Confessions*, ed. by P. Knöll and W. H. D. Rouse, trans. by William Watts, Loeb Classical Library, 2 vols (Cambridge, MA and London: Harvard University Press, 2006).

18. Goldin notes an implicitly Augustinian dimension to the *Lai de Narcisus*, which Guillaume likely knew, commenting: 'Amors "teaches" Narcisus, not by pouring previously unknown facts into his mind but by making him conscious of what is already there' (*Mirror*, pp. 41–42).

19. Gilbert, '"I am not he"', suggests that the *Rose* offers its readers 'alternative paths to fulfilment: erotic discourse may prove more appealing than sexual love' (p. 952).

20. I quote *Biblia Sacra iuxta Vulgatam Clementinam*, ed. by Alberto Colunga, OP and Laurentio Turrado (Madrid: Biblioteca de Autores Cristianos, 1965), with translations from the King James Bible.

21. As Sarah Kay explains, 'the masculine subject cannot form a relationship directly with the feminine, or vice versa. Instead, each connects only with objects that are merely indirectly related to the other subject, in the form of fantasies or symptoms', in *Žižek: A Critical Introduction* (Cambridge: Polity, 2003), p. 83. On Lacan's position, see Dylan Evans, *Dictionary of Lacanian Psychoanalysis* (London: Routledge, 1996), *q.v.* 'Sexual relationship (rapport sexuel)'. Evans notes

that Lacan's comment pertains to 'the relation between the masculine sexual position and the feminine sexual position' (p. 181).

22. See Fleming, 'Roman de la Rose', pp. 205–14.

23. See Kevin Brownlee, 'Jean de Meun and the Limits of Romance: Genius as Rewriter of Guillaume de Lorris', in Romance: Generic Transformation from Chrétien de Troyes to Cervantes, ed. by Kevin Brownlee and Marina Scordilis Brownlee (Hanover, NH: University Press of New England, 1985), pp. 114–34.

24. Fleming, with reference to the Epistle to the Romans, notes the 'witty play made of Pauline doctrines of grace' in Genius's sermon ('Roman de la Rose', p. 212).

25. See my 'Bodily Peril'; Kay, Place of Thought, pp. 180–85; Blumenfeld-Kosinski, Reading Myth, pp. 81–88.

26. See my 'Romance of the Rose', pp. 171–72.

27. See Winthrop Wetherbee, 'The Literal and the Allegorical: Jean de Meun and the "De Planctu Naturae"', Medieval Studies, 33 (1971), 264–91. Minnis, Magister amoris, notes that 'Jean problematizes rather than follows the prescriptive sexuality of De planctu naturae by intermingling the discourse of aggressive Ovidian eroticism' (pp. 107–08).

28. On Cadmus, see Jacqueline Cerquiglini-Toulet, 'Cadmus ou Carmenta: Réflexion sur le concept d'invention à la fin du Moyen Âge', in What is Literature? France, 1100–1600, ed. by François Cornilliat, Ullrich Langer and Douglas Kelly (Lexington, KY: French Forum, 1993), pp. 211–30.

29. See my 'Polytextual Reading: The Meditative Reading of Real and Metaphorical Books', in Orality and Literacy in the Middle Ages: Symbioses, Performances, Fictions, ed. by Mark Chinca and Christopher Young, Utrecht Studies in Medieval Literacy (Turnhout: Brepols, 2005), pp. 203–22; Eric Jager, The Book of the Heart (Chicago: University of Chicago Press, 2000).

30. 'Traictié d'une vision contre le Ronmant de la Rose', in Hicks, ed., Débat, pp. 59–87 (p. 79).

31. 'Traictié', p. 80.

32. Guynn asserts that 'the metaphorical climax is so powerful that it appears to explode all constraints [...] disrupting the relationship between signs and meanings' (Allegory, p. 150).

33. Col, 'Aprés ce que je oÿ parler'; Christine 'Pour ce que entendement', in Hicks, ed., Débat, pp. 98, 125. See my 'Confronting Misogyny: Christine de Pizan and the Roman de la Rose', in Translatio Studii: Essays by His Students in Honor of Karl D. Uitti for His Sixty-fifth Birthday, ed. by Renate Blumenfeld-Kosinski, Kevin Brownlee, Mary B. Speer and Lori J. Walters (Amsterdam and Atlanta, GA: Rodopi, 2000), pp. 169–87 (p. 181).

34. Kevin Brownlee notes that Jean's authorial stance combines 'clerkly bookish authority', 'experiential authority' and 'philosophical authority', in 'Reflections in the Miroër aus amoreus: The Inscribed Reader in Jean de Meun's Roman de la Rose', in Mimesis: From Mirror to Method, Augustine to Descartes, ed. by John D. Lyons and Stephen G. Nichols, Jr (Hanover, NH: University Press of New, 1982), pp. 60–70 (p. 69). See also Brook, 'Learning, Experience'; Erika Kanduth, 'Der Rosenroman — ein Bildungsbuch?' Zeitschrift für Romanische Philologie, 86 (1970), 509–24.

35. It has been argued that 'Guillaume de Lorris' and 'Jean de Meun' are different voices emanating from a single authorial figure; see Roger Dragonetti, 'Pygmalion ou les pièges de la fiction dans le Roman de la Rose', in Orbis Mediaevalis: Mélanges de langue et de littérature médiévales offerts à Reto Raduolf Bezzola à l'occasion de son quatre-vingtième anniversaire, ed. by Georges Guntert, Marc-René Jung, Kurt Ringger, Katharina Maier-Troxler and René Specht (Berne: Francke, 1978), pp. 89–111; Eva Martin, 'Away from Self-Authorship: Multiplying the "Author" in Jean de Meun's Roman de la Rose', Modern Philology, 96 (1998), 1–15. The prior and independent composition of Guillaume's poem, however, is supported by the existence of the anonymous continuation, by Gui de Mori's account of having encountered it on its own before his discovery of Jean's continuation, and by codicological evidence. See Hult, Self-fulfilling Prophecies, pp. 14–24, 36–40.

36. Kay, 'Sexual Knowledge', notes that 'The Rose both stages and inspires a massive programme of re-reading and questions our capacity to understand and learn from prior texts' (p. 85, emphasis hers).

CHAPTER 3

Orpheus's Songs (I)

The Failed Ascent and the Failure of Lineage

In the previous chapters, we have looked at ways that both Ovid and the authors of the *Rose* explore the complex relationship of sexuality and language. Animals, as noted by both Nature and la Vieille, engage unproblematically in an artless sexual coupling; but for humans, with their rational minds and fraught mixture of shame and desire, sexual relations are mediated by the screen of fantasy, language and law. Erotic desire is maintained through a self-consciously duplicitous game of revelation and concealment; and it is no surprise that Cupid takes an interest in poetry, a form of discourse that, like dream or fantasy, is simultaneously fictional and truthful. Poetic language transmits but does not reveal; it conjures the unspeakable and the ineffable by awakening memories and triggering associations in the mind of the reader. It creates a space apart within which fictionalized versions of both self and other — author and reader — can meet. Still, in that sense it also hinders any true 'face to face' encounter. The *Rose*, like other medieval allegorical texts, acknowledges the sexual, like the spiritual, as something that language may point towards, but can never fully represent.

In this chapter I wish to examine another set of figures from Ovid's *Metamorphoses*: Orpheus and the characters of whom he sings, in particular Pygmalion and his descendants. In these tales, poetic, musical and artistic powers are used in the service of erotic desires that transgress the heterosexual, reproductive norm: for the dead, for boys, for the father, for the inanimate representation of an idealized and impersonal femininity. Orpheus uses poetic discourse less as a vehicle of knowledge than for its affective power of persuasion and fantasy. Yet his spectacular performances always end in defeat. In the first half of his story — the descent into Hell in search of Eurydice — he is unable to fulfil his desire for what remains, in the end, an insubstantial image: reaching out to Eurydice as they near the edges of the upper earth, he sees her disappear, and 'nil nisi cedentes [...] arripit auras' [he clasped nothing but the yielding air] (*Met*. X, 59). In the second half, he is protected for a while by his song. Enraged by Orpheus's rejection of would-be female lovers in preference for adolescent boys, the Thracian women attack the bard. For a time, his song bewitches not only trees and animals, but even the projectiles hurled by his assailants. But in the end their shouts drown out his music; the magic circle is broken, and he is torn to bits.

Orpheus is mentioned only once in the *Rose*, when Genius calls for punishment of those who pervert Nature's work 'quant Orpheüs veulent ansivre' [when they choose to follow Orpheus] (*RR*, 19621): an echo of Alain de Lille's *De planctu naturae*, where Natura complains that 'solus homo, mee moderationis citharam aspernatus, sub delirantis Orphei lira delirat' (VIII, 54–55) [man alone turns with scorn from the modulated strains of my cithara and runs deranged to the notes of mad Orpheus' lyre (Pr. 4, p. 133)]. But Orpheus's relevance to the *Rose* goes beyond the local allusion to pederasty or other non-reproductive sexual behaviours. Given the powerful Boethian presence throughout Jean's continuation in particular, we can assume that medieval readers would also have had in mind Philosophy's retelling of Orpheus's descent into Hades (*CP* III, m. 12). In this well-known passage, often expanded in vernacular translations of the *Consolation*, Orpheus exemplifies the destructive nature of sensual desire.[1] Not only the motif of 'sterile' desire — that is, a desire that resists 'fruitful' liaisons with living women — but also those of excessive sensuality and the corrupting effects of lascivious art, poetry or music, offer parallels both to the Lover and to the figure of Narcissus against whom the Lover is defined. When Orpheus's most famous song, the tale of Pygmalion, Myrrha and Adonis, is retold by Jean de Meun, Pygmalion even compares himself to Narcissus, in that both fall in love with an inanimate image. Like Narcissus, these mythological figures have inspired extensive critical controversy as to whether they are meant as positive or negative reflections on the Lover and the duplicitous erotic discourse that he favours.

'Quis legem dat amantibus?'

Orpheus's lamentation has a powerful impact on all who hear it, inspiring a mimetic desire that cannot be withstood. Not in the sense that his listeners fall in love with Eurydice, or that they emulate his ideals in desiring an analogous object, but in an even more absolute manner. Forgetting their own torments, the entire population of Hell is gripped by the desire for Orpheus to recover Eurydice. But his song of love, bereavement and longing, even as it is being fulfilled, comes up against a rival discourse. As Ovid explains, Eurydice's presence is now circumscribed by prohibitions: 'hanc simul et legem Rhodopeius accipit Orpheus, / ne flectat retro sua lumina' [Orpheus, the Thracian, then received his wife and with her this condition, that he should not turn his eyes backward] (*Met.* X, 50–51). From one perspective Eurydice is a poetic effect summoned forth by the lyric persona of Orpheus's song, a construct of his desire. From the perspective of the gods, however, she is an offering defined within the parameters of the law — payment for a virtuoso performance. Orpheus is asked now to alter his performance, accepting new conditions for the staging of desire. Rather like Jean's 'Guillaume de Lorris', however, Orpheus is wholly identified with his desiring poetic persona, and is unable to maintain the necessary distance from that role.

How should we understand Orpheus's loss? Perhaps his desires were too great, exceeding the symbolic constructs that define sexual contact. He wanted true possession, when all that is possible is fleeting pleasure. Excessive desire is the failing that Virgil identifies in his account of Orpheus, through the words of Eurydice herself: 'illa "quis et me" inquit "miseram et te perdidit, Orpheu, / quis tantus furor?"' (*Georgics* IV, 494–95) [She cried: 'What madness, Orpheus, what dreadful madness, hath ruined my unhappy self and thee?'].[2] Ovid, however — with a wink to his illustrious predecessor — asserts that Eurydice had nothing with which to reproach her husband, since love itself cannot be a crime: 'iamque iterum moriens non est de coniuge quicquam / questa suo (quid enim nisi se quereretur amatam?)' [And now, dying a second time, she made no complaint against her husband; for of what could she complain save that she was beloved?] (*Met.* X, 60–61).

If anything, Ovid implies, it was not desire but lack of faith that thwarted Orpheus's quest: 'hic, ne deficeret, metuens avidusque videndi / flexit amans oculos' [he, afraid that she might fail him, eager for sight of her, turned back his longing eyes] (*Met.* X, 56–57). Unable to suspend disbelief, Orpheus requires visible proof; he condemns himself to a perpetual sense of loss by refusing to see that he is already whole. Eurydice lives on as a figment of Orpheus's imagination, and he can conjure her up poetically at any time; but he wants to possess her externally, in the flesh. Orpheus's predicament is similar to that of Narcissus, who also already had what he desired. As Ovid says, addressing Narcissus:

> quod petis, est nusquam; quod amas, avertere, perdes!
> ista repercussae, quam cernis, imaginis umbra est:
> nil habet ista sui; tecum venitque manetque;
> tecum discedet, si tu discedere possis! (*Met.* III, 433–36)

> [What you seek is nowhere; but turn yourself away, and the object of your love will be no more. That which you behold is but the shadow of a reflected form and has no substance of its own. With you it comes, with you it stays, and it will go with you — if you can go.]

The object of Narcissus's desire exists only as long as he is looking at it, but follows him wherever he goes; Eurydice exists, and follows her lover, only insofar as Orpheus does not look back at her. Both characters exemplify the inability of the imaginative fantasy, whether visually or poetically conceived, to measure up to the force of bodily desire.

Lacking detachment from his all-encompassing identity as lover, Orpheus is unable to negotiate the interface between the discourses of desire and prohibition. This aspect of the Orphean story is stressed in Boethius's account. As Philosophy comments when reminding Boethius of the singer's fate: 'Quis legem dat amantibus? / Maior lex amor est sibi' [Who can give lovers laws? / Love is a greater law unto itself] (*CP* III, m. 12, vv. 47–48). As the *Rose* in turn shows, love is subjected to a variety of laws: the prescriptions and prohibitions articulated by the major allegorical figures of the poem are all attempts to impose definitions and codes of behaviour on the mysterious force known as 'amors'. Whether it is the Ovidian *ratio* of carefully controlled seduction, the doctrine of Christian charity, or Nature's imperative to procreate — a process that, as she herself admits, also serves to channel the inheritance of wealth, power and status — the animal sex drive is crafted by the human intellect into a wide range of erotic discourses and performances. Yet none of these is ever wholly successful. And upon returning from his failed quest, in Ovid's account, Orpheus addresses precisely this issue.

In his second performance, the Ovidian Orpheus once again uses song to create a fantasy world of desire, this time in the form of a *locus amoenus* constituted by the many trees, birds and animals that are magically drawn by his music. Rather than trying to conjure Eurydice, however, Orpheus now creates a space within which to resist sexual attachments with women while enjoying the pleasures of pederasty, and his song is a tissue of forbidden desires:

> [...] puerosque canamus
> dilectos superis inconcessisque puellas
> ignibus attonitas meruisse libidine poenam. (*Met.* X, 152–54)

> [for I would sing of boys beloved by gods, and maidens inflamed by unnatural love and paying the penalty of their lust.]

Like Ovid himself — in a humorous moment of authorial identification with the famous bard — Orpheus renounces martial and imperial themes: 'cecini plectro graviore Gigantas / sparsaque Phlegraeis victricia fulmina campis' [I have sung the giants in a heavier strain, and the victorious bolts hurled on the Phlegraean plains] (*Met.* X, 150–51).[3] But his song also, implicitly, defines itself against his earlier performance in Hell — itself a form of gate-crashing not entirely dissimilar to that of the giants. Where formerly Orpheus staged his own desire, he now assumes the role of narrator, telling tales of other lovers. And where the earlier song sought to preserve and prolong conjugal love, the new one addresses rival forms of eros. Like Orpheus himself, however, most of the lovers of whom he sings are thwarted by fate or by chance, or punished for transgressing limits set by human law or divine decree.

If Orpheus seeks to protect himself within a veil of poetic fictions, then, he is still implicated in the tales that he tells, which are infused with his own desires and grievances.[4] Ganymede is the male love object that Jove succeeds in keeping, despite Juno's resistance — 'nunc quoque pocula miscet / invitaque Iovi nectar Iunone ministrat' [even now, though against the will of Juno, [Ganymede] mingles the nectar and attends the cups of Jove] (*Met.* X, 160–61) — just as Orpheus enjoys the favours of young men despite the jealousy of the Thracian women. Hyacinthus, another boy loved by a god, dies and is replaced by a symbolic memento: a recasting of Orpheus's loss of Eurydice in homoerotic terms. Moreover, Apollo kills Hyacinthus himself through his unfortunate discus toss, just as Orpheus 'killed' Eurydice with his fatal backward glance; and in both cases the perpetrator, being guilty only of love, feels himself blameless (*Met.* X, 61, 201). Pygmalion is granted sexual access to his beloved statue, but his final descendent, Adonis, also meets an untimely end, leaving Venus to grieve helplessly; like Apollo, she commemorates her lover with a flower. The tale of Hippomenes and Atalanta, finally, involves the triumph of love, followed by disaster when the lovers are turned into lions to punish their excessive lust.

Orpheus does succeed for a time in sustaining this poetic safe haven, but the fantasy eventually breaks down with the assault of the Maenads, who attack the bard with the cry 'hic est nostri contemptor!' [see the man who scorns us] (*Met.* XI, 7). The element excluded from Orpheus's pleasure-world — women — forces its way in and overwhelms him. In a sense, the discourse he had earlier disavowed

— the savage assault of the giants — also returns with a vengeance, as his poetry is drowned out by a cacophony of slander, rage and jealousy. Orpheus twice employs his songs in an effort to combat death; twice he fails, creating nothing more than poetic articulations of desire and loss.

Of all Orpheus's characters, the most important for the *Rose* is Pygmalion. Like Orpheus, Pygmalion rejects sexual liaisons with women; in an even more extreme move, he focuses his desire onto a purely imaginative screen, devoid of subjectivity. Like Narcissus, therefore, Pygmalion refuses potential lovers, only to fall for a visual image of idealized beauty.[5] The ivory of Pygmalion's image might even recall the 'eburnea colla' [ivory neck] (*Met.* III, 422) that Narcissus admired in his own reflected image. At the end Narcissus melts like wax — 'ut intabescere flavae / igne levi cerae' [as the yellow wax melts before a gentle heat] — and loses his rosy flush: 'neque iam color est mixto candore rubori' [no longer has he that ruddy colour mingling with the white] (*Met.* III, 487–88, 491). Pygmalion's statue also grows soft, 'ut Hymettia sole / cera remollescit' [as Hymettian wax grows soft under the sun] (*Met.* X, 284–85). But since she is coming to life rather than dying, she reverses the colour-change, as her once pale face blushes ('erubuit', v. 293) under Pygmalion's kisses. Presumably, then, Pygmalion succeeds where both Orpheus and Narcissus failed. And yet, as the lover of a work of art, he has succumbed even more fully to the seductive pull of fiction. At least Narcissus realized that he was in love with an insubstantial image, but Pygmalion imagines that his statue can be alive. Pygmalion is at once an idealization of the creative imagination and a parody of the elegiac poet proclaiming his love for the fictional Corinna.[6] Perhaps fittingly, his lineage turns in on itself, as if unable to escape the closed world of fantasy.

Myrrha, Pygmalion's ill-fated descendant, offers yet another variation on the Narcissan dilemma of erotic desire in a fundamentally non-erotic context.[7] Burning with passion for her father Cinyras, she laments that she cannot hope to possess him because he is already hers: 'quia iam meus est, non est meus, ipsaque damno / est mihi proximitas' [because he is mine, he is not mine; and [...] my very propinquity is my loss] (*Met.* X, 339–40). Myrrha's story is the culmination of Orpheus's song, introduced with dramatic warnings:

> dira canam; procul hinc natae, procul este parentes,
> aut, mea si vestras mulcebunt carmina mentes,
> desit in hac mihi parte fides, nec credite factum. (*Met.* X, 300–02)

> [A horrible tale have I to tell. Far hence be daughters, far hence, fathers; or, if your minds find pleasure in my songs, do not give credence to this story, and believe that it never happened.]

After expressing relief that his own homeland is innocent of such terrible crime, Orpheus stipulates that Myrrha's desire lay outside the domain of Cupid, resulting not from his arrows, but from the Furies. Myrrha herself experiences her incestuous desires as simultaneously delightful and abhorrent. She reflects that incest is practised by animals, whose freedom she envies — 'felices, quibus ista licent!' [happy they who have such privilege] — while lamenting the 'malignas [...] leges' [spiteful laws] that restrict human behaviour (*Met.* X, 329–30). She then imagines distant tribes who might permit sexual unions between parent and child, and longs to be one of them before recoiling from her fantasy: 'spes interdictae, discedite!' [Avaunt, lawless desires!] (*Met.* X, 336).

Incest is presented as something that violates language, placing words in positions that push the boundaries of sense. Remonstrating with herself, Myrrha exclaims: 'tune eris et matris paelex et adultera patris? / tune soror nati genetrixque vocabere fratris?' [Will you be the rival of your mother, the mistress of your father? Will you be called the sister of your son, the mother of your brother?] (*Met.* X, 347–48). Despite talking about it endlessly, Myrrha cannot articulate her desire openly. When her nurse demands the truth, the most she can manage is 'o [...] felicem coniuge matrem' [O mother, blest in your husband] (*Met.* X, 422) — enough, however, for the nurse to understand and enable the deed. Interestingly, Myrrha and her father do articulate their familial relationship during their fateful sexual encounter: 'forsitan aetatis quoque nomine "filia" dixit, / dixit et illa "pater", sceleri ne nomina desint' [It chanced, by a name appropriate to her age, he called her 'daughter', and she called him 'father', that names might not be lacking to their guilt] (*Met.* X, 467–68). Yet this open speech communicates nothing, as Cinyras remains oblivious to the truth of the words in that context. The reality of incest, it would seem, *cannot* be transmitted through direct speech, but only obliquely.

Ultimately Myrrha's desires so horrify her that she prays to be excluded from both life and death, 'ne violem vivosque superstes / mortuaque exstinctos' [lest, surviving, I offend the living, and, dying, I offend the dead] (*Met.* X, 485–86). She is consequently turned into a tree, losing her humanity altogether, although her despair continues to find symbolic expression in 'tears' of myrrh: 'quae quamquam amisit veteres cum corpore sensus, / flet tamen, et tepidae manant ex arbore guttae' [though she has lost her old-time feelings with her body, still she weeps, and the warm drops trickle down from the tree] (*Met.* X, 499–500). But where Myrrha's desires lay outside the artifice of eros, identifying her with fabled barbarian races and mindless bestial mating, her son is the very epitome of eroticized masculinity.[8] Pygmalion's final descendent, Adonis, becomes the lover of Venus herself, as the result of a curious incident: 'pharetratus dum dat puer oscula matri, / inscius exstanti destrinxit harundine pectus' [while the goddess's son, with quiver on shoulder, was kissing his mother, he chanced unwittingly to graze her breast with a projecting arrow] (*Met.* X, 525–26). A dangerous accident indeed, inviting the unspoken fantasy of a sexual liaison between Venus and Cupid — a possibility just barely foreclosed by the earlier assurance that Cupid's arrows do not spark incestuous desire. Adonis is hardly an innocent choice for Venus's affections under the circumstances, for he closely resembles Cupid: 'qualia [...] / corpora nudorum tabula pinguntur Amorum, / talis erat' [he looked like one of the naked loves portrayed on canvas] (*Met.* X, 515–17). Conceived in incest, Adonis becomes a screen to mask Venus's own incestuous longings: the substitute object that deflects her desires away from her own son.[9]

Pygmalion's sexual involvement with his erotic fantasy leads, then, to two forms of progeny: the myrrh tree and the anemone flower. The former embodies the unspeakable drives that lie outside the protective veneer of law, language and the artfully cultivated desires of Venus and Cupid. Its 'tears' of myrrh are a mute expression of the pain caused by the conflict between the bodily sex drive and the symbolic forms that attempt to constrain it. The other commemorates an idealized form of erotic desire, one through which the unspeakable desires of incest can be sublimated and disavowed — yet, ironically, one that is equally doomed to a tragic outcome. With its fragile blossoms — 'brevis est tamen usus in illo' [but short-lived is their flower] (*Met.* X, 737) — the flower that was Adonis commemorates the transience of pleasure, and the inevitability of loss.

'Pennas etiam tuae menti [...] adfigam'

While Jean drew primarily on Ovid's account of Orpheus and his songs, he was also influenced by medieval literary, philosophical and mythographic traditions. Two of Jean's most important sources, the *De planctu naturae* and the *Consolation of Philosophy*, capitalize on Orpheus's associations with both sexual excess or deviance, and a form of poetry as powerful as it is dangerous. In Boethius's work, Orpheus's song is contrasted not with the martial themes of epic, but with the discourse of philosophy. Philosophy introduces her tale of Orpheus with an articulation of the ideal — 'Felix qui potuit gravis / Terrae solvere vincula' [Happy who could loose the bonds / Of heavy earth] — and closes with an admonitory gloss: 'Quidquid praecipuum trahit / Perdit, dum videt inferos' [Whatever excellence he takes with him / He loses when he looks on those below] (*CP* III, m. 12: 3–4, 57–58). This framework makes very clear that Orpheus is a figure for the would-be philosopher-poet seeking intellectual and spiritual enlightenment — 'Quicumque in superum diem / Mentem ducere quaeritis' [[you] who seek to lead your mind / Into the upper day] (53–54) — and failing because of an inability to renounce earthly desires. For Boethius, Orpheus — like Ovid himself — represents a turning away from discourses of knowledge and enlightenment, in favour of the seductive but pernicious poetry of desire. It is from this backward movement that Philosophy saves Boethius, with her scathing attack on the *poeticas Musas* (I, pr. 1).[10]

The tale of Orpheus illustrates the lessons that Philosophy has been stressing throughout Book III: material wealth, public glory and bodily pleasure are false objects of desire that distract men from the pursuit of true, lasting happiness. Orpheus displays no interest in either wealth or fame, but even conjugal love, though somewhat sympathetically treated, is excluded from Philosophy's rigorous definition of the highest good.[11] In the closing poem of Book II, Philosophy praises love as a cosmic force. Beginning with its power to regulate nature, she moves on to the higher principle of human love:

> Hic et coniugii sacrum
> Castis nectit amoribus,
> Hic fidis etiam sua
> Dictat iura sodalibus. (II, m. 8, 24–27)

[And [love] ties the knot of holy matrimony / That binds chaste lovers, / Joins too with its law / All faithful comrades.]

Though conjugal love is a good thing, it is not the pinnacle of love in the sub-lunar world: that position is reserved for (presumably same-sex) friendship. Philosophy clarifies this point shortly thereafter, distinguishing friendship from marriage as both a higher good, and one that falls outside the domain of Fortune:

> uxor ac liberi quae iucunditatis gratia petuntur; amicorum vero quod sanctissimum quidem genus est, non in fortuna sed in virtute numeratur. (III, pr. 2, 33–35)

> [a wife and children are sought after for the pleasure they give; but the most sacred kind of good is that of friendship, a good reckoned not a matter of fortune but of virtue.]

The insufficiency of a wife and children to bring happiness is cited yet again in Book III, prose 7. When Philosophy finally concludes that Boethius has learned 'quae sit imperfecti, quae etiam perfecti boni forma' [what is the form both of the imperfect and of perfect good] (III, pr. 10, 1–2), it is clear that conjugal love has not been admitted into the latter category.

The two poems leading up to the Orpheus meter introduce imagery that sets the stage for his story. Meter 10 laments the nefarious lure of jewels and precious metals. Hidden in the depths of the earth, they serve only to distract from the true object of desire that is spiritual illumination:

> Hoc quidquid placet excitatque mentes,
> Infimis tellus aluit cavernis;
> Splendor quo regitur vigetque caelum,
> Vitat obscuras animae ruinas. (III, m. 10: 13–16)

> [Whatever that is that stirs men's minds with pleasure / The earth has cherished in its deepest caves. / The brightness by which the lively heavens are ruled / Shuns the soul's ruin and obscurity.]

Meter 11, in turn, is a reminder that although the corruption of the body has caused the mind to forget much of the spiritual wisdom it once had, this knowledge can still be accessed through internal contemplation:

> Non omne namque mente depulit lumen
> Obliviosam corpus invehens molem.
> [...]
> Quod si Platonis musa personat verum,
> Quod quisque discit immemor recordatur.
> (III, m. 11: 9–10, 15–16)

> [For the body weighing upon the mind with bulky oblivion / Has not removed all light: / [...] If Plato's muse rings true, / What each man learns, forgetful he recalls.]

Orpheus's search for an object of desire down in Hell and his devotion to sexual (albeit conjugal) love stand out in clear opposition to the themes of philosophically informed poetry. Orpheus journeys down into the darkness rather than up into the light; he seeks the wrong kind of treasure and strives to recover the wrong kind of memory. And as the allusion to Plato reminds us, he draws his inspiration from the wrong Muse.

The tale of Orpheus marks the end of Book III; the opening meter of Book IV rewrites Orpheus's erotic quest as a spiritual ascent. Here Philosophy offers to affix wings to the mind of her philosopher-pupil:

> Sunt etenim pennae volucres mihi
> > Quae celsa conscendant poli.
> Quae sibi cum velox mens induit,
> > Terras perosa despicit,
> Aeris inmensi superat globum
> [...]
> Quod si terrarum placeat tibi
> > Noctem relictam visere,
> Quos miseri torvos populi timent
> > Cernes tyrannos exules. (IV, m. 1: 1–5, 27–30)

> [For I have wings swift flying / Which can ascend the heights of heaven; / When your quick mind has put them on, / It looks down on the hated earth, / Passes beyond the sphere of measureless air/ [...] / But if you like to look upon / Earth's night that you have left, / Those tyrants wretched people fear as fierce / You will see as exiles.]

The gender positions are reversed as the female Philosophy guides the male Boethius to an imaginary vantage point from which he can gaze back down on the tiny speck of the earth. As in Philosophy's gloss on the tale of Orpheus, the mind ascends on the wings of intellectual discourse. And the backwards glance does no harm if it is informed by insight into the transience of earthly power, where the human soul languishes in exile from its celestial abode. It is not the simple fact of looking, then, but the corrupting force of bodily desire — powered by a poetic of eros and lamentation — that blights the soul's ascent.

'Puis je voler avec les grues?'

In Jean's portion of the *Rose*, motifs associated with the Boethian Orpheus inform the Lover's encounter with Reason.[12] Citing both Boethius and Pythagoras, Reason points out that Heaven, not earth, is the soul's true home (*RR*, 4995–5010). In approximately a quarter of all surviving *Rose* manuscripts, the so-called 'litany of love' interpolation has Reason urging the Lover not merely to intellectual enlightenment, but to a mystical ascent achieved through the power of spiritual love.[13] Though Reason does not offer the Lover philosophical 'wings', her affinities with Philosophy and her citation of Boethius could easily conjure this image in the mind of an attentive reader. The Boethian intertext, in fact, must be taken into account in order fully to understand the Lover's objections to Reason's teachings. In his first substantial intervention after her citation of Boethius, the Lover adopts the image of flight:

> Puis je voler avec les grues,
> voire saillir outre les nues,
> con fist li cignes Socratés?
> [...]
> li dieu cuideroient espoir

> que j'asaillisse paradys
> con firent li geant jadis,
> s'en porroie estre foudroiez. (*RR*, 5393–95, 5398–5401)

[Can I fly with the cranes, indeed leap above the clouds, as did the swan of Socrates? [...] The gods might think I was assaulting Heaven, as did the giants long ago, and I could be struck down with a thunderbolt.]

The 'swan of Socrates' is Plato; the expression derives from an anecdote in John of Salisbury's *Policraticus* (II, 16), in which Socrates realizes that his dream of a high-flying swan referred prophetically to the arrival of his most promising pupil.[14] The Platonic swan, and the implicit Boethian image of ascent, trigger the Lover's other ornithological image: *grues*, or cranes. Reason herself mentioned cranes nearly a thousand lines earlier, with her use of the idiom 'prendre au ciel la grue' [pluck the crane from the sky] (*RR*, 4417) — to perform an impossible task — in reference to the monastic vow of chastity.[15] Both that expression and the Lover's adaptation of it draw their force from the ability of cranes, as noted in bestiary tradition, to fly at extreme heights. The Lover's comment, subtly recalling Reason's acknowledgment of the difficulties entailed in a vow of chastity, reflects his view that she demands an unacceptably rigorous standard of detachment from worldly concerns. In one stroke the Lover replies both to Reason and to the Boethian text that informs Reason's arguments, rejecting the counsel of 'Plato's muse' along with an imagined intellectual ascent on metaphoric wings.

The image employed by the Lover takes on further significance in the light of other traits assigned to cranes in bestiary tradition. In addition to flying at exceptional heights, cranes are said to form a perfect society in which each member knows his duty and performs it impeccably. The standard allegorical reading of cranes is given by Hugh of Fouilloy in his twelfth-century *Aviarium*:[16]

> Grues cum de loco ad locum transvolant ordinem procedendi volando servant. Illos autem significant qui ad hoc student ut ordinate vivant. Cum autem ordinate volando procedunt, ex se litteras in volatu fingunt: illos autem designant qui in se Scripturae praecepta bene vivendo formant. (p. 202)

> [When cranes fly from one place to another, they maintain a flight formation. They symbolize, moreover, those who strive to live by the Rule. Moreover, when they fly in formation they fashion letters with their bodies as they fly: further, they denote moreover those who by righteous living form within themselves the teachings of Scripture.]

'Flying with the cranes' thus implies soaring on intellectual wings to a vantage point beyond the reach of Fortune — the task at which the 'swan of Socrates' excelled but at which Orpheus, and evidently also the Lover, failed. And it implies belonging to a perfectly rational society, in which the individual is part of a collective effort to stage Scriptural teachings with one's very body — the community of those who accept Reason as their *amie*.

The Lover, unsurprisingly, takes a dim view of 'flying with the cranes': for him, it is perilously close to repeating the crime of the giants who attempted to scale Olympus. His allusion to the giants is also informed by the omnipresent Boethian intertext, echoing an exchange between Boethius and Philosophy in the Prose immediately preceding the 'Orpheus' Meter. There Boethius, grasping Philosophy's proof that the supreme Good rules all things, rejoices that the misconceptions that have been tormenting him are finally dispelled. Philosophy's reply is striking: '"Accepisti," inquit, "in fabulis lacessentes caelum Gigantas; sed illos quoque, uti condignum fuit, benigna fortitudo disposuit"' ['You have read in stories,' she said, 'of the giants challenging heaven; but those too, as was wholly right, a kindly strength put in their proper place'] (*CP* III, pr. XII, 69–71). In Philosophy's formulation, the giants' assault is analogous to the ignorance that clouds the human mind, while the victorious gods correspond to the powers of reason. By implication, Orpheus's attempt to bring sexual pleasures along with him in his ascent towards the light is analogous to the giants' bodily assault on Heaven. The Boethian intertext, so powerfully visible throughout the discourse of Reason as elsewhere in the *Rose*, deflates the Lover's argument even as he makes it; for it is of course his resistance to Reason — and not his potential acceptance of her advice — that makes him, like Orpheus, comparable to the combative giants of old.

If the Lover's logic fails to hold up within the Boethian context that defines Reason's line of argument, however, it is draws strength from the larger intertextual network in which their debate takes place: on the one hand, the Ovidian context that defines his amorous quest, and on the other, that of the *Policraticus*, evoked in his allusion to the 'cignes Socratés' [swan of Socrates] (*RR*, 5395). As we have seen, Ovid presents his *Amores* as an alternative to singing of the war between the gods and the giants; and the Lover now intimates that abandoning the erotic stance outlined by Ovid would somehow mean embracing the hubris of the giants, as if these two positions really were mutually defining opposites. The intertextual presence of the *Policraticus*, in turn, clarifies what this return to the giants might mean. Reason argues forcefully for the wisdom of the pagan philosophers — citing Socrates as a particularly apt role model (*RR*, 5817, 6150, 6857, 6880) — and asserting that 'il fet bon croire les paians / con de leur diz granz biens aians' [it is good to believe the pagans, as we can derive much good from their sayings] (*RR*, 7031–32). But the Lover is suspicious. If Reason wants him to emulate Socrates or his 'swan' Plato, he implies, she is exposing him to the fate of pagan philosophers who, according to John of Salisbury, believed too much in their own intellectual powers:[17]

> Quasi ergo mole gigantea subuecti et iam non humanis uiribus roborati intumuerunt indixeruntque bellum gratiae Dei de uigore rationis et libero confisi arbitrio [...] Deiecti sunt itaque dum alleuarentur, et dicentes se esse sapientes stulti facti sunt. (*Pol.*, VII, 1; vol. II, p. 94)

> [As though therefore with the bulk of giants, with strength no longer human, they became swollen with pride and proclaimed war against the grace of God with the strength of their reason and with confidence in the freedom of their will [...] They were therefore cast down even as they were being raised up, and professing themselves to be wise they became fools. (Pike, 217)]

John's condemnation of the pagans forms a convenient screen for the Lover's anxieties — an unthreatening explanation for his evocation of the giants just a few lines after citing John's 'swan' anecdote. And yet it does not seem enough to account for his dramatic reaction. It is his devotion to a pagan god, Cupid, and not a supra-rational Christian faith, that pits him against Reason. If the giants embody the intellectual hubris of those who believe too much in rational powers, they carry a further association that, for the Lover, would be even more sinister. In Book III, John of Salisbury bemoans male prostitution and transvestism as an offence against nature: 'In ipsam naturam, quasi gigantes alii teomachiam nouam exercentes, insurgunt' (III, 13; vol. I, p. 219) [they rise against nature herself like a new set of giants waging a new war against heaven (Pike, 200)].[18] And it is here, I believe, that we get to the heart of the Lover's covert, but most pressing, objection to Reason's arguments.

The Lover, whose biases are not subtle, stigmatizes Reason's proposal of 'ne soi quele amor sauvage' [I know not what uncivilized love] (RR, 5347) as a reversion from courtly refinements to rustic crudeness — a lapse into the worst excesses of pagan pride and degeneracy. His comment further implies that abandoning his love for the Rose might lead — as happened with Orpheus — to a redirection of desire towards male love objects. Though Reason's comments on conjugal love are more favourable than those of Philosophy, it is not marriage that she recommends to the Lover, but rather 'amistiez' [friendship] and a kind of all-purpose charity: 'Tu peuz amer generaumant / touz ceus du monde leaumant' [you can, in a general way, loyally love everyone in the world] (RR, 4655, 5417–18).[19] In the context of a confrontation between Boethian rationalism and Ovidian eros, the ambiguous echo of the *Policraticus* allows the Lover to hint at an identification of homoeroticism with the celibate lovers of Reason.

In redefining the choice that Reason attempts to offer him, the Lover locates himself in an intertextual space defined not only by Ovid and John of Salisbury, but also by Alain de Lille's *De planctu naturae*.[20] In this latter text, whose presence is particularly strong in the discourses of Reason and Nature, the principal opposition is not between the frenzy of desire and the serenity of *souffisance*, but between same-sex and opposite-sex eroticism. And while it may seem comically wilful of the Lover to cling to this distinction in the face of Reason's arguments, his position is not entirely foreign to medieval clerkly culture. In 1402, defending the *Rose* against charges of immorality, Pierre Col notes that 'les euvres de Nature' [Nature's works] are legitimate 'pour continuer l'espesse humainne et pour delaisser l'euvre contraire a nature, qui est abhominable a plus exprimer' [to continue the human species and to avoid the act contrary to nature, which it is an abomination to articulate any further].[21] Nature's work in the perpetuation of the species might seem an end in itself, not merely a means of distraction from the non-reproductive 'abominations' — autoerotic, homoerotic or otherwise — that threaten to consume the human race. Nonetheless, procreative heterosexual activity could be defined on some level as a bulwark against these unspecified and unspeakable acts. Who knows what might follow in the wake of its renunciation? Such, at any rate, are the anxieties implicit in the Lover's protestations. And it is to this aspect of the Lover's quest that I now turn.

Notes to Chapter 3

1. On the adaptations and glosses of the Orpheus poem in medieval French translations of Boethius, see Atkinson and Babbi, eds, *Orphée*. On Orpheus in Boethius and the medieval commentary tradition, see Friedman, *Orpheus*, pp. 86–145.
2. All citations and translations of the works of Virgil are to *Eclogues, Georgics, Aeneid*, ed. and trans. by H. Rushton Fairclough, Loeb Classical Library, 2 vols (Cambridge, MA: Harvard University Press; London: William Heinemann, 1969).
3. As noted in Chapter 1, the war between the giants and the gods was the subject of the epic that Ovid supposedly set out to write before being sidetracked by Cupid into composing the *Amores* (*Am.* I.i). See Karl Galinsky, 'Ovid's Poetology in the *Metamorphoses*', in *Ovid: Werk und Wirkung. Festgabe für Michael von Albrecht zum 65. Geburtstag*, ed. by Werner Schubert, 2 vols (Frankfurt-am-Main: Peter Lang, 1999), I, 305–14 (pp. 310–12).
4. Kathryn L. McKinley notes that the stories 'suggest Orpheus' inner landscape', in *Reading the Ovidian Heroine: Metamorphoses Commentaries, 1100–1618* (Leiden: Brill, 2001), p. 27. Hardie, *Ovid's Poetics*, sees them as 'a celebration of Orpheus's love for his dead wife' (p. 65). John F. Makowski, arguing that Orpheus loses interest in Eurydice after her second death, sees the tales as dominated by 'pederastic and misogynist themes', in 'Bisexual Orpheus: Pederasty and Parody in Ovid', *The Classical Journal*, 92 (1996), 25–38 (p. 29).
5. Hardie, *Ovid's Poetics*, characterizes Orpheus's tale of Pygmalion as 'a pendant to the story of Narcissus' in the larger context of the *Metamorphoses* (p. 189).
6. See Galinsky, 'Ovid's Poetology', p. 312.
7. On Myrrha, see McKinley, *Reading the Ovidian Heroine*, pp. 34–42.
8. Dragonetti, 'Pygmalion', comments that 'De l'inceste de Mirra et de son père [...] la beauté poétique donnera lieu à cette nouvelle figure qui a nom Adonis' [From the incest of Mirra and her father [...] poetic beauty will give rise to this new figure whose name is Adonis] (p. 109).
9. See Hardie, *Ovid's Poetics*, pp. 187–88.
10. On the importance of Orpheus and Ovid for Boethius's persona, see Claassen, 'Literary Anamnesis'; Anna Crabbe, 'Anamnesis and Mythology in the *De consolatione philosophiae*', in *Atti. Congresso internazionale di studi Boeziani, Pavia 5–8 ottobre 1980*, ed. by Lucia Obertello (Rome: Herder, 1981), pp. 311–25; Seth Lerer, *Boethius and Dialogue: Literary Method in the 'Consolation of Philosophy'* (Princeton, NJ: Princeton University Press, 1985), pp. 153–59, 172–75; Lucken, 'Muses', pp. 149–51.
11. See Claassen, 'Literary Anamnesis', pp. 6, 12.
12. On Jean's use of Boethius, see Langlois, *Origines*, pp. 136–38; Ott, 'Jean de Meun und Boethius'.
13. See my *'Romance of the Rose'*, pp. 164–67; for the text of the 'litany', see pp. 365–68. On this passage's distribution in *Rose* manuscripts, see Ernest Langlois, *Les Manuscrits du Roman de la Rose: Description et classement* (Lille: Tallandier; Paris: Champion, 1910), p. 425.
14. Fleming, *Reason and the Lover*, pp. 127–29. See also Langlois, *Origines*, p. 148. Citations of the *Policraticus* are from *Policratici, sive De nugis curialium et vistigiis philosophorum, Libri VIII*, ed. by Clemens C. I. Webb, 2 vols (Oxford: Clarendon Press, 1909); translations are from *Frivolities of Courtiers and Footprints of Philosophers: Being a Translation of the First, Second, and Third Books and Selections from the Seventh and Eighth Books of the Policraticus of John of Salisbury*, by Joseph B. Pike (Minneapolis: University of Minnesota Press, 1938).
15. See Rowe, 'Reson', p. 110.
16. I cite *The Medieval Book of Birds: Hugh of Fouilloy's 'Aviarium'*, ed. and trans. by Willene B. Clark (Binghamton, NY: Medieval and Renaissance Texts and Studies, 1992).
17. The analogy of the giants is also applied to physicians, with their suspect curiosity about the secrets of nature; see *Policraticus* II, 29.
18. On John's treatment of sexual 'perversion' in the *Policraticus*, see Burgwinkle, *Sodomy*, pp. 71–73.
19. On Reason's comments about marriage, see my *'Romance of the Rose'*, pp. 169–70.
20. On Jean's use of Alain, see Langlois, *Origines*, pp. 148–50.
21. 'Aprés ce que je oÿ parler', in Hicks, ed., *Débat*, p. 107.

CHAPTER 4

Orpheus's Songs (II)
Poetry, the Unspoken and the Unspeakable

In the *Consolation of Philosophy*, Orpheus figures as one who failed to escape the clutches of Hell; Philosophy's focus is not on his supposed invention of pederasty, but on the lack of moral discipline that caused him to look back in desire. His motivations in seeking Eurydice were impure. Orpheus's moral failings are reflected in his misuse of poetry, as a discourse of desire rather than as one of enlightenment. Most literally, he lost the 'good' of conjugal love when he corrupted it with lust. More abstractly, he failed to recognize his marriage as one of the insubstantial gifts of Fortune, and refused to accept his loss; in so doing he exiled himself from the higher plane of philosophical serenity. Philosophy's gloss on the Orpheus myth is less fitting to the Ovidian Orpheus, than to that of Virgil's *Georgics*. There, Orpheus's failure on the ascent is attributed not to a fear that Eurydice might fail him, as in Ovid's account, but to forgetfulness: the fault that afflicts the human mind as, burdened by the flesh, it struggles to recover the knowledge it once had. In Virgil's words: 'restitit, Eurydicenque suam iam luce sub ipsa / immemor, heu! victusque animi respexit' [He stopped, and on the very verge of light, unmindful, alas! and vanquished in purpose, on Eurydice, now his own, looked back] (*Georgics* IV, 490–91). Virgil's account — like that of Boethius's Philosophy — makes no mention of Orpheus's pederasty, nor of fantastic tales told in a wondrous grove. Instead, his Orpheus embraces a barren and lonely existence, endlessly telling and retelling the story of his loss:

> solus Hyperboreas glacies Tanaimque nivalem
> arvaque Rhipaeis numquam viduata pruinis
> lustrabat, raptam Eurydicen atque inria Ditis
> dona querens. (*Georgics* IV, 517–20)

> [Alone, he would roam the northern ice, the snowy Tanais, and the fields ever wedded to Rhipaean frosts, wailing Eurydice lost, and the gift of Dis annulled.]

From the moralizing perspective of Philosophy, Orpheus never does leave the domain of Hell, even if he technically climbs back out onto the surface of the earth. The Virgilian Orpheus, gripped by *dementia* (488) and *furor* (495), forgetful of the truth, intensifying his grief in the lamentations of his song, is even closer to the sorrowful Boethius than his Ovidian counterpart.

If Philosophy's poem evokes the Virgilian Orpheus, however, readers of Boethius would certainly have known the Ovidian Orpheus as well, and the somewhat different sexual 'crime' for which he was killed: not (or not merely) abstinence from sexual liaisons through devotion to the dead, but the one with which he is identified by Alain de Lille, namely the redirection of erotic desire from women to boys.[1] Both the homoeroticism of Orpheus and the divergent readings implied by different versions of his story, are at issue in the debate between Reason and the Lover: a passage in which the consolations and chastisements of Boethian Philosophy are closely interwoven with the complaints and lamentations of Alain's Natura.

'Spernitur ipsa'

Though the Lover never mentions Orpheus by name, his disinterest in an intellectual 'ascent' and his unbending commitment to Cupid associate him with the Boethian reading of Orpheus's failed quest. Orpheus is also implicitly evoked in Reason's warning to the Lover when she asks him to accept her as his *amie*: 'Trop sunt dolentes et confuses / puceles qui sunt refusees' [maidens who are spurned are all too sorrowful and humiliated] (*RR*, 5804–05). Reason's explicit point is that the Lover should not repeat the self-absorbed, delusional desires of Narcissus, as defined by Guillaume de Lorris: a man cursed by the noble lady whose love he spurned. But Reason's words also associate Narcissus — and the Lover — with Orpheus, that other famous victim of *puceles refusees*. From Reason's perspective, this association would only strengthen her point: just as Narcissus gazed obsessively down at his own image rather then looking up to God, so Orpheus turned back towards Hell in sensual longing, rather than focusing on the light above. The self-absorbed isolation described by Virgil, that single-minded obsession with a figure conjured up through song, does have a Narcissan quality. Both men failed to follow Reason; both were targeted by female avengers who might be seen as executing a just punishment.

There is something disconcerting, however, about Reason's argument. The Lover is not normally thought of as one who refuses the attention of maidens; quite the opposite. Mystified by Reason's excessively erudite language, he asks her to clarify her request, 'non en latin, mes en françois' [not in Latin, but in French] (*RR*, 5810). From the Lover's Ovidian perspective, the crime of both Narcissus and Orpheus was, quite literally, to have repudiated women as love objects. And yet this seems precisely what Reason urges him to do even as she cautions him against the vengeful passions of 'puceles qui sunt refusees'. Her advice, adapted from Alain's Natura, is unconditional flight from erotic love: 'ne peuz bevre si bon bevrage / conme penser de lui fouir' [you cannot drink such a good draught as to think in terms of fleeing it] (*RR*, 4324–25). More than ten thousand lines later, Genius will use very similar terms in warning men to be on their guard against feminine wiles: 'riens n'i vaut herbe ne racine, / seul foïr an est medecine' [neither herb nor root is of any use there; the only cure is flight] (*RR*, 16585–86). But as if suddenly aware of the potential implications of this advice, Nature's priest hastily qualifies his words:

> Si ne di je pas toutevoie,
> n'onc ne fu l'antancion moie,

> que les fames chieres n'aiez
> ne que si foïr les daiez
> que bien avec eus ne gisiez. (*RR*, 16587–91)

[Still, I'm in no way saying — such was never my intention — that you should not cherish women, nor that you should flee them to such an extent that you don't lie with them.]

Reason, like Genius, also acknowledges that heterosexual love is acceptable within the context of marriage and procreation. Of couples joined in proper, reasonable love, she says:

> Ne cuides pas que jes dessenble:
> je veil bien qu'il aillent ensanble
> et facent quant qu'il doivent fere
> conme courtais et debonere. (*RR*, 4559–62)

[Don't think that I would separate them: I do want them to come together and do what they need to do, in a courteous and noble way.]

Since marriage is not part of the Lover's agenda, however, and Reason at no point tells him that it should be, her allowance for conjugal love carries little force. What she stresses is hostility to Cupid, the god whose service robs men of 'sens, tens, chatel, cors, ame, los' [sense, time, belongings, body, soul, reputation] (*RR*, 4598). Far from urging the Lover to marry, she chastises him for neglecting his studies: 'Tu mez en livres ton estuide, / et tout par negligence oblies!' [you study books, and then through your negligence you forget it all!] (*RR*, 6754–55).

Reason's advice might lead the Lover to immerse himself in a male community defined by shared literary and aesthetic interests; yet this trajectory is one that excludes women just as surely as the homoerotic liaisons and autoerotic pleasures of Orpheus or Narcissus. If fealty to Cupid is a deflection from some other path, just what are those paths not taken? As we have seen, the formative model of Narcissus, the phallic description of the *bouton* and the Lover's obsession with Bel Acueil destabilize the overtly heterosexual discourse of the text; alternative desires are never completely out of view. The unspoken presence of Orpheus that informs the Lover's encounter with Reason contributes to the process by which the quest for the Rose is defined in dialogue not only with la Vieille's commodification of sex and with Reason's promotion of philosophical study, but also with both homosocial and homoerotic desire.[2]

Reason excludes homosexuality from the many forms of love that she describes. Her definition of erotic love, borrowed from Andreas Capellanus, identifies 'amors' as something that springs up between two people 'de divers sexe' [of opposite sex] (*RR*, 4347–50). Homoerotic liaisons — rather like incest in Orpheus's song of Myrrha — lie beyond the reach of Cupid:[3]

> Touz li mondes va cele voie,
> c'est li dex qui touz les devoie,
> se ne sunt cil de male vie
> que Genius exconmenie
> pour ce qu'il font tort a Nature. (*RR*, 4311–15)

[The whole world goes that way — he is the god who leads everyone astray — except those evil-doers whom Genius excommunicates because they wrong Nature.]

Reason is careful to point out that she is in favour of procreation, and acknowledges that sexual pleasure is a natural phenomenon meant to ensure the propagation of the species. What she criticizes is the lover's devotion to pleasure as an end in itself:

> qui veust d'amors joïr sanz faille,
> fruit i doit querre et cil et cele.
> [...]
> Mes l'amor qui te tient ou laz
> charnex deliz te represente,
> si que tu n'as ailleurs entente.
> Por ce velz tu la rose avoir. (*RR*, 4516–17, 4570–73)

[Whoever wants to enjoy the pleasures of love must without exception — male or female — seek its fruit [...] But the love that holds you in its snares offers you carnal delights, so that you think of nothing else. That's why you want the rose.]

Throughout this tirade, Reason delicately avoids the question of sexual relations between men, which must also be motivated by pleasure rather than procreation. Whatever the behaviour of Genius's excommunicants may be, Reason is not prepared to see it as love, nor is she prepared to discuss it. She comments only that her condemnation of their behaviour does not imply approval of Cupidinous love:

> ne pour ce se je n'ai d'els cure
> ne veill je pas que les genz aiment
> de cele amor, dom il se claiment
> en la fin las, chetif, dolant. (*RR*, 4316–19)

[Just because I don't like them, doesn't mean that I want people to love according to this love that will, in the end, make them feel worn out, wretched and sorrowful.]

But despite Reason's disclaimer that damning one possible choice does not imply praise for its opposite, the Lover promptly accuses her of preaching hatred:

> Puis qu'amors ne sunt mie bones,
> ja mes n'ameré d'amors fines,
> ainz vivrai toujorz en haïnes?
> Lors si seré mortex pechierres. (*RR*, 4618–21)

[Since love is no good, I'll never experience refined love, so will I always live in a state of hatred? In that case I'll be a mortal sinner.]

Reason is clearly piqued by this accusation, for she returns to it on two occasions (*RR*, 5341–44, 5696–97). The Lover's comments spark an argument in which Reason protests yet again that just because she condemns one thing does not mean that she recommends an even greater folly in its place: lovers should not turn to hatred, any more than spendthrifts should turn to avarice (*RR*, 5699–5720). This particular question, in fact, leads to some quite unseemly bickering: 'Je ne faz pas tex argumanz. / — Si fetes voir. — Certes tu manz' [I'm not making any such claim. –You are so. –You're certainly lying] (*RR*, 5721–22).

Given Reason's earlier comments, this peculiar altercation could be a coded way of addressing the question of whether Cupidinous love is a greater or a lesser folly than its other 'opposite', homoerotic liaisons: whether it is worse, that is, to seduce maidens or to spurn them altogether. Reason's concern here is not with the wrongs done to women by pleasure-seeking men, but solely with the integrity of the male subject, defined through his relations with a feminine that slips between the human and the allegorical. Though she borrows the trope of the 'spurned maiden' and compares herself to Echo, her point is to offer herself in substitution for an erotically defined *amie*. As a grammatically feminine love object, she remains just barely appropriate to a heterosexual framework, but strictly within the realm of allegory. For the Lover, however, the pursuit of the female love object is a means of constructing his male identity; as Ami advises him, 'cuillez la rose tout a force / et moutrez que vos estes hon' [pluck the rose by force and show that you're a man] (*RR*, 7660–61). A purely allegorical relationship — with his own rational faculty, no less — sounds to him suspiciously close to the very behaviour for which Narcissus was chastised. And the requisite disinterest in the sexual love of maidens inevitably raises the spectre of a different form of erotic desire. Might this, rather than hatred, be the 'mortal sin' to which the Lover is really referring?

The implicit anxiety about homoeroticism is intensified through Reason's kinship with Alain's Natura, with whom she shares not only similarities but also crucial differences. Reason's intervention in Jean's continuation, and her condemnation of the Lover's lamentations, have obvious Boethian echoes, borne out in the philosophical content of her tirade. Her opening gambit with the Lover, however — the long oxymoronic 'description of love' — is borrowed from the *De planctu naturae*, inviting comparisons with Natura (*RR*, 4263–4328; *De planctu*, VIII [Prose 4], 260–76, and IX [Meter 5]). In the opening meter of the *De planctu*, Alain's persona laments the prevalence of male homoeroticism and the resulting scandal of *puceles refusees*:

> Spernitur ipsa tamen, quamuis decor ille peroret
> Et forme deitas disputet esse deam.
> [...]
> Virginis in labiis cur basia tanta quiescent,
> Cum reditus in eis sumere nemo uelit?
> Que michi pressa semel mellirent oscula succo,
> Que mellita darent mellis in ore fauum.
> (De planctu, I, 37–38, 43–46)

[She herself is despised, though that fair face may carry the day and her godlike form maintain that she is a goddess [...] Why do so many kisses lie fallow on maidens' lips while no one wishes to harvest a crop from them? If these kisses were but once planted on me, they would grow honey-sweet with moisture, and grown honey-sweet, they would form a honey-comb in my mouth. (Meter I, pp. 70–71)]

Alain's persona in fact has two grievances: not just the sexual habits of his male companions, but also the fact that he cannot benefit as much as he would like to from the abundance of unclaimed maidens. His heterosexual interests exclude him from those targeted by Genius's excommunication, and the allegorical lady who appears at his moment of need is far less concerned with his re-education than is the case with Philosophy's consolation of Boethius, or Reason's chastisement of the Lover. Indeed, Natura's consolation of Alain's persona is expressed in surprisingly erotic terms. Philosophy contented herself with drying Boethius's tears, but Natura goes considerably further, granting Alain's persona the pleasures he had been longing for: 'meque suis innectendo complexibus meique ora pudicis osculis dulcorando mellifluoque sermonis medicamine a stuporis morbo curauit infirmum' (*De planctu* IV, 8–10) [Entwining me in an embrace and sweetening my lips with chaste kisses, she cured me of my illness of stupor by the medicine of her honey-sweet discourse (Pr. 3, p. 116)]. Natura's subsequent 'complaint' touches on incest, prostitution and adultery; but her principal grievance is with male homosexuality.[4] Though Natura regrets Cupid's excesses and gently chastises Alain's persona for his attachment to this figure, she is far more worried about the havoc wrought by his bastard half-brother, Jocus. Indeed, she is almost apologetic about her criticisms of Cupid, feeling a need to explain herself:

> Nec mirandum si in pretaxata Cupidinis depinctione notulas reprehensionis intersero, quamuis ipse michi quadam germane consanguinitatis fibula connectatur. (*De planctu* X, 2–5)

> [You must not be surprised that in the foregoing description of Desire I have interjected some items of censure despite the fact that he is connected with me by a certain bond of true companionship. (Pr. 5, p. 154)]

Natura has, after all, appointed Venus as her deputy in the sublunar realm, entrusting her, along with her husband Hymen — Natura's own brother — and their son Cupid, with the perpetuation of life on earth (*De planctu* VIII [Prose 4], 240–46).

Small wonder, in short, that the Lover is confused by a tirade that cautions him against scorning the love of maidens, while also advising him at length to flee the power of Cupid. Reason inverts Natura's priorities, making only a passing reference to same-sex desire while portraying the dangers of heterosexual eroticism in hyperbolic terms. For a self-styled *amie*, Reason has a bit too much philosophical austerity. Far from kissing the distraught Lover, she does not even stoop to dry his eyes. She lacks both the feminine allure of Natura, and her partnership with Venus; she dismisses Cupid out of hand. As if haunted by the intertextual presences of Narcissus, Orpheus and the sodomites condemned by John of Salisbury and Alain de Lille, the Lover strikes back: So what about the alternative, then... the opposite of heterosexual love? Isn't that a mortal sin?

'Cortaise parole'

One might ask why, if the Lover is so concerned with the possibility or appearance of homoerotic desire, he does not simply say so. But of course 'plain speech' about sex is not his style, and the topic of euphemism and figurative language provides a further point on which he and Reason can disagree, as well as an additional way in which Reason falls short of the feminine graces displayed by Natura. As is well known, Reason's disinterest in courtly euphemism and the aestheticization of sex leads to her casual use of the word *coilles* [testicles]; the word first occurs in her account of the castration of Saturn, which she briefly relates in arguing the subordination of justice to charitable love (*RR*, 5507–08). When the shocked Lover demands to know why Reason did not gloss the offending term 'par quelque cortaise parole' [with some courteous expression], he notes that the things she has so explicitly named 'ne sunt pas bien renomees / en bouche a cortaise pucele' [are not well-reputed in the mouth of a courteous maiden] (*RR*, 6905, 6900–01): thereby creating an implicit image of oral sex that, as David Hult has noted, is more obscene than the merely verbal crime of which Reason stands accused.[5] Earlier, as we have seen, the Lover insinuated that Reason's advice to flee Cupid might lead to other, unspeakable, sexual practices. And now the terms of his complaint not only identify Reason with un-ladylike language, but also, through the verbal sleight-of-hand, juxtapose a parable about castration with an image of non-reproductive sex. Though that latter association remains implicit at this point, it will become explicit in the discourse of Genius, who opens with a resounding condemnation of those who fail to engage in procreative sex, arguing that they deserve castration; identifies the Heavenly Park that welcomes those who do procreate with the Golden Age of Saturn's reign, as it existed before Jupiter's act of castration; and indulges in a forty-six-line condemnation of castration as another impediment to procreation, before continuing with his main line of argument. While the Lover does not share Genius's interest in procreation, he does manifest a similar tendency to collapse distinctions between the behaviours that lie outside of his own sexual ethos.

The Lover's reprimand of Reason echoes Natura, who used similar language in explaining her reluctance to speak openly of homosexuality:

> In sequenti tamen tractatu, ne locutionis cacephaton lectorum offendat auditum uel in ore virginali locum collocet turpitudo, predictis uiciorum monstris euphoniae orationis uolo pallium elargiri. (*De planctu*, VIII, 192–95)

> [In the following disquisition, however, it is my intention to contribute a mantle of fair-sounding words to the above-mentioned monsters of vice to prevent a poor quality of diction from offending the ears of readers or anything foul finding a place in a maiden's mouth.[6] (Pr. 4, p. 144)]

Natura, after all, is the last one who would want anything like *that* in her honeyed mouth. The Lover's squeamishness also recalls another of the Latin sources for his discussion with Reason, as does his confidence that obscenity is permitted if one is merely citing someone else: 'Mes des que je n'en sui fesierres, / j'en puis bien estre recitierres' [but as long as I'm not the one to initiate it, I can certainly quote it] (*RR*, 5687–88).[7] In the *Policraticus*, John acknowledges that homosexuality might be best passed over in silence, but justifies himself by noting that it was explicitly addressed in the New Testament:

> Verum haec abominatio non tam ostendenda est quam conspuenda, puderetque eam nugis nostris esse insertam, nisi eandem Apostolus Romanis scribens uerbis manifestius expressisset, dicens quia [...] masculi, relicto naturali usu feminae, exarserunt in desideriis suis, masculi in masculos inuicem turpitudinem operantes. (III, 13; vol. I, pp. 219–20)

> [Such abomination should be spat upon rather than held up to view, and I would have been ashamed to insert an account of it in this work had not the

> Apostle, in his epistle to the Romans, written even more explicitly on the theme, [saying that] 'the men, also leaving the natural use of women, have burned in their lusts one toward another, men with men working that which is filthy'. (Pike, 200)]

John's quotation of Romans 1. 26–27 is a more explicit articulation of same-sex eroticism than anything he felt able to express in his own words, and in that sense is analogous to the Lover's willingness to remind Reason that 'ci m'avez coilles nomees' [here you named testicles in my presence] (*RR*, 6899). Reason, however, is not speaking of sodomy (or fellatio) — topics she seems just as happy to avoid — and she hastens to clarify that in her mind genitals are wholly identified with procreation: 'car volentiers, non pas enviz, / mist Dex en coillons et en viz / force de generacion' [for willingly, not unwillingly, God placed the power of generation in the testicles and the penis] (*RR*, 6935–37). Indignantly, she points out that she is perfectly free to speak of 'chose qui n'est se bone non' [something that is purely good] (*RR*, 6918).[8] It is not the members themselves that are morally good or reprehensible, but what one does with them — and that evidently comes down to the question of whether they are put to use in the interests of generation or of pleasure.

Reason's efforts to enlighten the Lover about the literal and allegorical uses of language echo Natura's reprimand to Alain's protagonist, who wonders why men are castigated for their homoerotic indulgences when, according to poetic tradition, the gods engage in much the same behaviour. In both poems the naïve protagonist receives a lesson on 'les integumanz aus poetes' [the integuments of the poets] (*RR*, 7138). Natura reminds her young charge that 'poete sine omni palliationis remedio auditoribus nudam falsitatem prostituunt' (*De planctu*, VIII, 128–29) [poets present falsehood, naked and without the protection of a covering, to their audience (Pr. 4, p. 139)]. Poetic fictions may indeed offer philosophical teachings; but only 'exteriori falsitatis abiecto putamine dulciorem nucleum ueritatis secrete intus lector inueniat' (Ibid., 134–36) [when the outer shell of falsehood has been discarded the reader finds the sweeter kernel of truth hidden within (Ibid., p. 140)]. Or as Reason puts it: 'La verité dedenz reposte / seroit clere, s'el iert esposte' [the truth hidden within would be clear if it was expounded] (*RR*, 7135–36). Though the divine sexual 'crime' that sparks the argument in the *Rose* is castration rather than homoeroticism, the terms of the discussion are remarkably similar.

Reason's encounter with the Lover, then, is richly informed not only by Philosophy's instruction of Boethius, but also by the condemnations of pleasure-seekers elaborated by both John of Salisbury and Alain de Lille. The spectre of vain, excessive or non-reproductive desire haunts the moral critique of erotic love as well as the debate about language. Natura's principal concern is with legitimate lines of descent, leading her to take an interest both in the choice of love-object, and in the social context of the encounter. Since marriage is the necessary precondition for the reconstruction of natural procreation into socially meaningful lineage, she opposes all forms of sexual activity that lie outside this frame: homoerotic acts are obviously excluded, but so are heterosexual fornication, incest, adultery and prostitution. For Reason, sexual relations are likewise permitted if they are motivated by the desire for offspring and performed within the institution of marriage, but her real recommendation is the redirection of desire into intellectual study. Since her focus is on the distinction between sexual pleasure and affairs of the mind, the identity of the sexual love-object is largely irrelevant to her discussion. The Lover, however, is more concerned with the erotic tensions of the quest and the means of passing beyond this stage to achieve sexual consummation; as Reason rightly notes, his goal is pleasure, not marriage or the production of an heir. And since the pursuit of pleasure could involve a love-object of either sex, the distinction between same-sex and opposite-sex desire becomes more crucial. The Lover's construction and defence of his identity as lover circle endlessly round the forbidden topic of homoeroticism, while leaving it largely unacknowledged.

'Sub delirantis Orphei lyra delirat'

It falls to Genius, as I have said, to address a sexual ethics that is based not on sexual pleasure as such, but on its subordination to the procreative imperative. Yet even he cannot openly name the behaviour that he wants to condemn. Nature herself uses the term 'sodomite' in a long list of human failings (*RR*, 19204), but Genius does not speak so directly. Rather than referring explicitly to Orpheus's fabled resistance to women, Genius expresses his criticism through the three metaphors central to his discourse of sexual procreation: he complains that Orpheus 'ne sot arer ne escrivre / ne forgier en la droite forge' [did not know how to plough or write or forge in the proper forge] (*RR*, 19622–23). Genius's accusation is not without humour. Although Orpheus was a consummate master of poetry, his medium was song, and he had the power to rearrange entire landscapes simply by singing; he was indeed neither writer nor ploughman. As a result of Genius's circumlocutions, Orpheus is associated with a desire that produces no progeny, be it homoerotic, autoerotic or necrophiliac; with a failure to operate the technologies of farming and manufacturing that impose a cultural order on raw nature; and with lyricism rather than the written word, with its capacity to spawn glosses, new readings and new texts. As one of those excluded from the Park, he is implicitly associated with the idle pleasure-seeking of Deduit's garden and with Narcissus. Like Narcissus as he is depicted in the *Rose*, Orpheus spurned women; like Echo, those women took their revenge. Like Deduit, who imported trees from distant lands to construct a space for desire and song, Orpheus's music creates an arboretum in which he sings.[9] There, surrounded by trees that are in some cases doomed lovers themselves, Orpheus abandons himself to the erotic pleasure of his own poetic discourse.[10] In this way too he resembles Narcissus, who called upon the woods to witness his grief in an amorous liaison that had no existence outside the lament in which he tried to call his beloved *puer* into being.[11]

If Reason critiques the Lover's devotion to pleasure, then, Genius targets a different problem; but in both cases Orpheus, together with Narcissus, lurks as the negative model that must be overcome. Reason's Boethian teachings implicitly warn the Lover not to re-enact Orpheus's failure to detach from carnal desires, or Narcissus's rejection of morally acceptable love objects. And she steers him away from the literal reading of poetry that is exemplified in Narcissus's love for a reflected image, or Orpheus's performance in Hell: an obsession with surface imagery, a desire for words as things. Genius focuses most explicitly on the other pitfall that Orpheus, like Guillaume's Narcissus, embodies — the refusal of heterosexual liaisons — while also condemning the use of poetic language to create a dream-like world of fantasy and desire, in which procreative sexual fulfilment is forever blocked. Whether he is joining in the static lyricism of the carol, dallying in sterile pleasures with the male Bel Acueil, or dwelling on a fictional object of desire that always exceeds his grasp, the Lover has come perilously close to recreating the poetic isolation of Narcissus or Orpheus, sealed in a protective bubble of erotic fantasy.

It is not only in his wooing of Bel Acueil and his private lamentations that the Lover substitutes language for action; he also experiences the pleasure of *Douz Parler* [Sweet Talk] in his encounters with Ami. The God of Love prescribed these conversations about 'la bele qui ton cuer emble' [the beautiful girl who steals your heart] (*RR*, 2680) with a male companion as a means of relieving the torments of desire. But if they are too successful, these delightful discussions risk prolonging the state of desire forever, as heterosexual love becomes a means of male homosocial bonding. A humorous hint of this possibility seeps through in Ami's allusion to Theseus and Pirithous as a model of ideal friendship. In classical mythology, Theseus accompanied Pirithous into Hell in his unsuccessful attempt at abducting Proserpine. In Ami's version, however, Theseus descends to Hell in search of Pirithous himself, after the latter's death:

> tant le queroit, tant le sivoit,
> car cil dedenz son queur vivoit,
> que vis en enfer l'ala querre,
> tant l'ot amé vivant seur terre. (*RR*, 8121–24)

> [He sought him and followed after him so much, for that one lived in his heart, that he went alive to seek him in Hell — so much had he loved him when he was alive on earth.]

Jean does not imply a sexual relationship between Theseus and Pirithous; still less, between Ami and the Lover.[12] But this striking model of an Orphic figure seeking his male love object in Hell does hint at the possibility that male friendship might short-circuit Cupid's model in such a way as to eliminate the lady altogether, or at least render her irrelevant. Even if maidens are not spurned outright, they are still in danger of being reduced to little more than a medium of male bonding. From Cupid's perspective, this might not pose a problem, since the ongoing process of *Douz Parler* will still produce a satisfying flow of love poetry. But from Genius's perspective, it is vital to ensure that the Lover does not lose himself in the pleasures of language to such an extent that he fails to translate erotic discourse into procreative action.

Both Reason and Genius, then, criticize the Lover for languishing in a state of protracted desire. Both offer advice about how to attain Heaven, the soul's true home. Reason counsels him to escape the vagaries of Fortune by renouncing erotic love, and thereby to attain the serenity of *souffisance*. Genius, however, targets less the pain of desire than its self-indulgent pleasures: not the *charnel delit* condemned by Reason, but the pleasure of desire itself. Uninterested in Fortune, he identifies the enemy as Atropos, or bodily death. The solution that he proposes is not serenity but hard labour: desire must give way to sexual consummation, which in turn must be of the kind that produces lineage. Reason wants the Lover to be a better reader, moving from body or letter to spirit; Genius wants the Lover to be a more active writer, endlessly enclosing the spirit within a series of new fleshly bodies.

'Ceste amour [...] ne vient mie de Nature'

If Orpheus himself is a largely implicit presence in the *Rose*, certain characters from his song play a far more prominent role: Pygmalion and his descendants, Myrrha and Adonis.[13] Jean's retelling of these tales introduces a number of modifications. In his version, Pygmalion's love for the statue is far more anguished than in Ovid's telling. There is nothing in the *Metamorphoses* to compare with the tortured monologues of Jean's Pygmalion, who resembles the Ovidian Myrrha in that regard. Like her, he is traumatized by his desires, reflecting that 'ceste amour est si horrible / qu'el ne vient mie de Nature' [this love is so horrible that it does not come from Nature] (*RR*, 20832–33). Jean's Pygmalion absorbs the tainted aura of 'unnaturalness' that Ovid identified with Myrrha, whose incestuous passion is passed over far more rapidly in the *Rose*. Omitting all of Myrrha's soul-searching, Jean shifts much of the blame onto her elderly nurse, whose machinations blighted Cinyras's otherwise happy reign. In the *Rose*, Mirra's story thus presents a royal lineage devastated by the meddling of an old duenna, archenemy of patriarchal law and order. We know that the *Rose*'s own Vieille, like Ovid's Myrrha, envies the indiscriminate sexual mating of animals, and chafes under the laws that regulate human sexual activity. Pygmalion, however, turns not to some conniving old woman, but to Venus. The juxtaposition of his story with that of Mirra supports the contrast, played out in the *Rose* overall, between Venus and la Vieille as two forms of female desire, both of which resist male regulation, but one of which is nonetheless more compliant with male desire than the other.

Though Jean's Pygmalion contrasts himself with Narcissus, his protestations highlight their similarities.[14] And he admits to being worse than men who pine for unattainable women: at least their love objects are capable of a favourable response. From Genius's perspective, it makes little difference whether we view Pygmalion in terms of celibacy, autoeroticism or homoeroticism. Indeed, rather like the Lover's *bouton*, the statue has a subtly phallic quality, being 'autresinc roide / conme est uns pex' [as stiff as a post] (*RR*, 20873–74). Its chilling effect on Pygmalion's mouth when he attempts to kiss it — 'toute me refredist la bouche' [it totally chills my mouth] (*RR*, 20876) — carries a submerged expression of revulsion at the prospect of oral sex, rather like that hinted at in the Lover's earlier comment to Reason about *coilles* in the mouth of a maiden. Pygmalion's musical wooing of the statue, without precedent in the Ovidian text, heightens still more his conformance to the desires condemned by Genius. Jean's description of Pygmalion's antics is an amusing piece of wordplay:

> puis prent freteaus et refretele;
> et chalumeaus, et chalumele;
> et tabor et fleüste et tymbre,
> et tabore et fleüste et tymbre;
> et cythole et tronpe et chevrie,
> et cythole et tronpe et chevrie;
> et psalterion et vïele,
> et psalterione et vïele. (*RR*, 21013–20)

[Then he takes a *fretel* and flutes on it; and a pipe, and pipes; and a drum and flute and tambourine, and drums and flutes and plays the tambourine; and a citole and trumpet and bagpipe, and strums and trumpets and pipes, and a psaltery and a fiddle, and he plays the psaltery and fiddles.]

Several of the noun-verb pairs found here suggest, in their appearance, masculine and feminine forms of the same word: *freteaus-refretele, chalumeaus-chalumele, tabor-tabore, psalterion-psalterione*. A visual illusion of masculine and feminine pairing, in other words, dissolves as we realize that all we are really seeing is a man's solo production of music from a series of inanimate objects; what looked like a feminine noun is in fact a verb whose subject is Pygmalion himself. Jean's verbal play is probably inspired by Alain de Lille's association of grammatical and sexual 'perversions' in the opening meter of the *De planctu Naturae*: 'Predicat et subicit, fit duplex terminus idem, / Grammatice leges ampliat ille nimis' (I, 19–20) [He is subject and predicate: one and the same term is given a double application. Man here extends too far the laws of grammar (Meter 1, p. 68)]. Pygmalion's obsessive music-making is an autoerotic fantasy, not unlike Orpheus's songs, Narcissus's monologues or Deduit's endless carolling. In all cases, the result is an avoidance of the 'writing' that Genius demands. Though Jean's Pygmalion asks Venus's forgiveness for his long devotion to 'chastée' [chastity] (*RR*, 21053–78), his behaviour with the statue would hardly count as chaste by any normal understanding of that term. 'Chastity' here serves as a euphemistic cover for erotic fantasies and behaviours that are not directed at women — in Pygmalion's own words, a love outside the domain of Nature. Once again, celibacy is implicitly associated with other non-reproductive sexual behaviours.

Jean's treatment of Pygmalion and his progeny is further complicated by a structural peculiarity: the story of Adonis, Pygmalion's final descendent, precedes the stories of Pygmalion and Mirra by some five thousand lines.[15] Jean alludes to the birth of Adonis in describing the liaison of Cinyras and Mirra — 'li beaus Adonys an fu nez' [the fair Adonis was born from that] (*RR*, 21172) — but asserts that continuing any further with that story would be a digression from the matter at hand: 'Ne vos veull or plus ci tenir, / a mon propos doi revenir, / qu'autre champ me convient arer' [I don't want to keep you on this matter any longer, I need to get back to my main subject, for I have other fields to plough] (*RR*, 21185–87). By this point in the poem, the image of ploughing is far from innocent; one cannot help thinking of Genius's exhortations, 'Arez, por Dieu, baron, arez' [plough, for God's sake, barons, plough] (*RR*, 19671). If we attribute the above comment to the authorial voice, it is a banal metaphor for the completion of the poem. But if we associate it with the Lover, it reminds us that it is time to abandon these Orphic tales, and get on with the business of sexual gratification.

The moral that Jean draws from the death of Adonis is that a man must always believe his *amie*, whether or not she is telling the truth: 'S'el jurent: "Toutes somes vostres", / creez les conme paternostres' [If they swear: 'We are entirely yours', believe them like the Our Father] (*RR*, 15727–28). The Lover clearly takes this lesson to heart when Bel Acueil grants him the Rose:

> Ne sai s'il fist puis d'avantages
> autant aus autres conme a moi;
> mes bien vos di que tant l'amoi
> que je ne le poi onques croire,
> neïs se ce fust chose voire. (*RR*, 21630–34)

> [I don't know if he later granted such privileges to others as he did to me; but let me tell you, I love him so much that I can't believe he did, even if it was true.]

Here the Lover distinguishes himself not only from Adonis, but also from the Ovidian Orpheus. Seeking proof of the lady's fidelity, looking back to ensure that she never falters — 'ne deficeret metuens' [afraid that she might fail him], in Ovid's words (*Met.* X, 56) — can only be a recipe for disaster. It might even lead to the loss of heterosexual desire. The Lover has learned that if one sort of fantasy can obstruct sexual desire, fantasy of another sort is essential to its fulfilment. His penetration, with Venus's help, of a feminine statue suggests that he is re-enacting the fantasy of Pygmalion's success with his statue, and the Lover believes this fantasy for all he is worth.[16] He will not fall into the perverse music-making that kept Orpheus and Pygmalion locked in the grip of unrequited desire, but engages energetically in the activity promoted by Genius:[17]

> car, Dieu merci, bien forgier sai.
> Si vos di bien que plus chiers ai
> mes .II. martelez et m'escharpe
> que ma cithole ne ma harpe. (*RR*, 21343–46)

> [For, thank God, I do know how to forge. I tell you that I consider my two hammers and my staff far more precious than my citole or my harp.]

No danger, in short, of the Lover being side-tracked into those unspeakable acts that, according to Genius, prove a man unworthy of his *coilles*.

The rearrangement of the Ovidian narrative means that if one did want to continue from Pygmalion and Mirra to the story of Adonis, it would be necessary to return to an earlier point in the text, from which one would carry on through the complaint and 'confession' of Nature, the discourse of Genius, and the story of Pygmalion and Mirra with its invitation to return to Adonis... an endless loop that promises yet again to block the Lover's progress towards the Rose. Can it be coincidence that it is the song of Orpheus that creates this 'bubble' of poetic resistance to the Lover's triumphant insemination of the Rose?[18] On the surface, or edges, of this bubble are tales of incest and 'unnatural' love; inside it we find the lamentations of Nature and Genius's condemnation of the (unnamed) Orphic sin. Only by turning his back on these alternative desires, and silencing his doubts about the female love object, can the Lover finally create himself as a heterosexual being.

Only by breaking out of this closed circle — by resisting the desire for a backward glance — can the combined erotic and poetic projects be completed.

Notes to Chapter 4

1. For a comparative discussion of Ovidian and Virgilian treatments of Orpheus, with particular attention to the question of pederasty, see Makowski, 'Bisexual Orpheus'.

2. Kevin Brownlee argues that Jean separates Orpheus's identity as pederast from that of poet, in 'Orpheus' Song Re-Sung: Jean de Meun's Reworking of *Metamorphoses*, X', *Romance Philology*, 36 (1982), 201–09 (p. 207). Susan Schibanoff sees a more ambivalent treatment of Orpheus in the *Rose*, in 'Sodomy's Mark: Alan of Lille, Jean de Meun, and the Medieval Theory of Authorship', in *Queering the Middle Ages*, ed. by Glenn Burger and Stephen F. Kruger (Minneapolis: University of Minnesota Press, 2001), pp. 28–56. On the Orphic coupling of inspired poetry and sexual deviance in Ovid, Jean de Meun and Chaucer, see Michael A. Calabrese, '"Make a Mark That Shows": Orphean Song, Orphean Sexuality, and the Exile of Chaucer's Pardoner', *Viator*, 24 (1993), 269–86. Guynn notes that 'both homoerotic and homosocial desire in the *Rose* work to stabilize a clerical ideology predicated on male solidarity and the exclusion and subordination of women' (*Allegory*, p. 195, n. 62).

3. Guillaume's Cupid distances himself from homoerotic desire; in a passage adapted from Ovid (*Ars* I, 523–24), he admonishes the Lover not to use make-up, as this should be left to women 'ou a cels de mauvés renon, / qui amors par male aventure / ont recovrees sanz droiture' [or to those ones of ill-repute who have illegitimately acquired love through evil means] (*RR*, 2160–62). Numerous manuscripts read 'Ont trovees contre Nature' for Lecoy's v. 2162, as reflected in Langlois's edition, v. 2174.

4. See Burgwinkle, *Sodomy*, pp. 170–99; Guynn, *Allegory*, pp. 93–135. Burgwinkle suggests that 'Alain's argument [...] was part of a body of topoi in circulation which were understood to deprecate same-sex eroticism' (*Sodomy*, p. 182).

5. Hult, 'Language and Dismemberment: Abelard, Origen, and the *Romance of the Rose*', in *Rethinking the 'Romance of the Rose': Text, Image, Reception*, ed. by Kevin Brownlee and Sylvia Huot (Philadelphia: University of Pennsylvania Press, 1992), pp. 101–30 (pp. 116–17). On this passage more generally, see also Fleming, *Reason and the Lover*, pp. 105–12; Hult, 'Poetry', pp. 32–35; my *'Romance of the Rose'*, pp. 107–08; Kelly, *Internal Difference*, pp. 44–51; Minnis, *Magister amoris*, pp. 125–28; Daniel Poirion, 'Les Mots et les choses selon Jean de Meun', *Information littéraire*, 26 (1974), 7–11; Maureen Quilligan, 'Words and Sex: The Language of Allegory in the *De planctu Naturae*, the *Roman de la Rose*, and Book III of *The Faerie Queen*', *Allegorica*, 1 (1977), 195–216.

6. I have slightly amended Sheridan's translation.

7. Fleming takes this to mean that the Lover cannot use an obscene word of his own invention, but is free to use those invented by someone else; see *Reason and the Lover*, pp. 101–03. I read this passage, however, as meaning that he is free to use the offending words only in reference to someone else's usage or in speaking of the words themselves as objects; see my *'Romance of the Rose'*, pp. 179–80.

8. Pierre Col makes this point in 'Après ce que', in Hicks, ed., *Débat*, p. 96.

9. Oiseuse explains to the Lover that Deduit 'de la terre Alixandrins / fist ça les arbres aporter / qu'il fist par le vergier anter' [caused the trees to be brought from the land of Alexander (i.e. the exotic East) so as to graft them onto the orchard] (*RR*, 590–92).

10. Kay, *Place of Thought*, notes that the pine, cypress, laurel and myrrh — all of whom figure in other Ovidian myths — are among the trees drawn by Orpheus's music (p. 66).

11. '"Ecquis, io silvae, crudelius" inquit "amavit"' [Did anyone, O ye woods, ever love more cruelly than I?] (*Met.* III, 442).

12. Minnis notes that the Lover's relationships with both Ami and Bel Acueil might be understood in terms of '"male bonding" of a kind which is characterized by fear, and indeed hatred, of homosexuality' (*Magister Amoris*, p. 205).

13. On these figures in the *Rose*, see Brownlee, 'Orpheus's Song' and 'Pygmalion, Mimesis'; Kelly, *Internal Difference*, pp. 76–81.

14. On parallels between Pygmalion and Narcissus in the *Rose*, see McCaffrey, 'Guillaume de Lorris'. For readings that contrast these two figures, see Brownlee, 'Pygmalion, Mimesis'; Gunn, *Mirror of Love*, pp. 286–90; Hill, 'Narcissus, Pygmalion'; Minnis, *Magister amoris*, pp. 105–07; Poirion, 'Narcisse et Pygmalion'; and my *From Song to Book*, pp. 86–99.

15. The story of Venus and Adonis occupies *RR*, 15647–734; that of Pygmalion and his descendants through Myrrha occurs at *RR*, 20787–1180.

16. Thérèse Bouché notes that the closing episode of the poem is 'la réécriture, dans un autre registre, de l'"exemplum" de Pygmalion', in 'L'Obscène et le sacré, ou l'utilisation paradoxale du rire dans le Roman de la Rose de Jean de Meun', in *Le Rire au moyen âge dans la littérature et dans les arts*, ed. by Thérèse Bouché and Hélène Charpentier (Bordeaux: Presses Universitaires de Bordeaux, 1990), pp. 83–95 (p. 90).

17. Orpheus's instrument is normally portrayed as stringed, most commonly *lyra* (Ovid, Alain) or *harpe* (*Ovide moralisé*, Machaut). The citole is one of the instruments played by Jean's Pygmalion.

18. Brownlee notes that the stories of Pygmalion and his descendants are the only Ovidian myths recounted by Jean's narrator in his own voice, giving them special prominence; see 'Orpheus's Song', pp. 201, 207–08.

CHAPTER 5

The Conquest of the Rose

A Virgilian 'Art of Love'?

In the foregoing pages we have seen many examples of how the *Rose* tantalizes its readers with the promise of knowledge. The *art d'amors* is laid out in considerable detail; yet any certainty about its ultimate import always seems to dissolve on a close reading. The Orphic tales discussed in the last chapter, for example, may imply that it is best to forge unhesitatingly onward, suppressing all doubts about the virtue of one's *amie*; yet this policy might also be seen as inviting the betrayal visited upon the unsuspecting Cinyras. At the heart of the uncertainties besetting the poem is its treatment of women. The *Rose* posits 'woman' as an object of both desire and knowledge, while also portraying her as infinitely gifted in her powers of resistance and evasion, deception and obfuscation.[1]

The refusal to resolve these dilemmas is one of the means by which the *Rose* resists unity of meaning. In this final chapter, I turn to the concluding section of the poem, examining the questions raised by a series of Virgilian citations.[2] Bracketing the final battle for the Rose, the tales of Adonis, Pygmalion and Mirra, and the discourses of Nature and Genius, are allusions to both the *Aeneid* and the *Eclogues*. In the initial skirmishes, Seürtez taunts Poor as unsuited to battle, citing her role in Cacus's cowardly flight when he was attacked by Hercules (*RR*, 15543–58; *Aeneid* VIII, 205–24). Later, when the Lover is forcing his way through the narrow opening that leads to the Rose, he compares himself to Hercules dislodging the boulder that blocked the entrance to Cacus's cave (*RR*, 21589–602; *Aeneid* VIII, 225–32). Within that frame is a second set of Virgilian citations. In his antifeminist tirade, Genius paraphrases a warning from *Eclogue* III: 'Qui legitis flores et humi nascentia fraga, / frigidus, o pueri, fugite hinc, latet anguis in herba' (92–93; *RR*, 16556–64) [Ye who cull flowers and low-growing strawberries, away from here, lads; a chill snake lurks in the grass]. And after the conflagration in the Tower, Courtoisie advises her son, Bel Acueil, to let the Lover take the Rose, citing *Eclogue* X: 'omnia vincit Amor: et nos cedamus Amori' (69; *RR*, 21297–303) [Love conquers all; let us, too, yield to Love]. Inside this framework are three further Virgilian citations. Genius quotes the *Aeneid* (IV, 569–70) in warning men to be on their guard against women (*RR*, 16295–99); in his sermon, he paraphrases Virgil's account of the decline of the Golden Age (*Georgics* I, 125–46; *RR*, 20085–150). Finally, Nature notes that Virgil was rewarded with land in Naples, as well as citing his supposed prophecy of Christ in *Eclogue* IV, 7–9 (*RR*, 18697, 19139–46).[3] Both la Vieille and the Jaloux also allude to the *Aeneid* (*RR*, 8978–82, 13144–80, 13438–44). It is primarily with Genius, however, and with the Lover's accession to the Rose, that this chapter will be concerned.

The symmetrical structure created by these citations both questions and celebrates the Lover's success. The mock heroic frame of Herculean battle, one might say, propels him through the series of Orphic myths that stand between him and the Rose. The inner frame of *Eclogue* citations first raises the troubling spectre of feminine betrayal, but then defuses that danger with the affirmation of love triumphant. The Virgilian presence implies a critique of the Lover's sensuality and grandiosity, but one that is resisted by the Ovidian tenor of the poem.[4] Even some of the allusions to Virgil or his writings turn out, on closer examination, to be Ovidian citations. In stressing the dangers of drink and of falling asleep in inappropriate places, for example, la Vieille cites Palinurus, who fell asleep at the helm (*RR*, 13438–44; *Aeneid* V, 838–61), as well as briefly recounting the tale of Dido. Her familiarity with the *Aeneid* might seem improbable; but Virgil's epic is among the works that Ovid counsels women to read in the *Ars* (III, 337–38). La Vieille's Virgilian citations thus reflect her thoroughly Ovidian make-up, as do her readings themselves. Rather than following medieval commentary tradition in viewing Palinurus as the 'wandering vision' or 'roving eye' that brought Aeneas to Carthage but must be eliminated if he is ever to reach Italy,[5] la Vieille prefers to keep Palinurus awake as the 'helmsman' of sexual adventuring. And of course she sees Dido not as a pernicious obstacle in Aeneas's path to glory, but as a tragically wronged woman: a thoroughly Ovidian reading best represented in the *Heroides*. Nature's comment about the honour once shown poets and the land bestowed on Virgil and Ennius paraphrases yet another Ovidian passage (*RR*, 18689–702; *Ars* III, 405–12); even this praise of Virgil is really a quotation of the licentious art of love. The interplay of Ovidian and Virgilian perspectives on love and sexuality forces the reader to question once again just what kind of knowledge is ultimately imparted by the *Miroër aus Amoureus*.

'Varium et mutabile semper femina'

In his Apology to female readers, Jean states that his unflattering portrayal of women is essential to his pedagogical aims. The knowledge of feminine wiles is beneficial for men and women alike:

> Mes por ç'an escrit les meïsmes
> que nous et vos de vos meïsmes
> poïssons connoissance avoir,
> car il fet bon de tout savoir. (*RR*, 15181–84)

[But we put it in writing so that both we [men] and you [women] can know all about you, for it is good to know everything.]

Yet the discourse of la Vieille, the warnings offered by Genius, and the misogynistic commentary elaborated by Ami both in his own voice and in that of the Jaloux, paint a uniformly bleak picture of the feminine 'love object' as anything but lovable. The ideals represented by the arrows of love soon seem hopelessly naïve.

Cortoisie — if she was ever anything other than a screen for devious behaviour — is all but eclipsed by Dangier. Simpleice is belied by la Vieille's revelations, and by Bel Acueil's disingenuous behaviour as he pretends to enjoy her company, feigning ignorance and disinterest in love (*RR*, 12541–52, 14578–92). The fifth arrow, Biau Semblant, morphs into Faux Semblant, who serves women just as readily as men.[6] It might be tempting to conclude that the more a man knows about women, the less capable he will be of heterosexual desire.

This paradox is less resolved than simply sidestepped. Women are inherently duplicitous, and men should be on their guard; at the same time, they are encouraged to embrace a fantasy of feminine compliance. As Orpheus shows, looking over one's shoulder to confirm the fidelity of one's *amie* only creates the possibility of witnessing her fall from grace, ominously followed in his case by a preference for male love objects. Vulcan exemplifies the dangers of attempting to control a woman's sexual behaviour; as la Vieille comments, he would have been better off not laying snares, 'mes feinsist que riens n'en seüst / s'il vousist avoir bele chiere / de Venus, que tant avoit chiere' [but he should have pretended not to know anything if he wanted the good will of Venus, whom he cherished so much] (*RR*, 14154–56). One way of understanding this might be to say that a man can have either rational knowledge of the female character or carnal knowledge of the female body; but perhaps not both at once. And since the former brings pain while the latter brings pleasure, the choice may seem clear. As Jean's narrator says in his gloss on the Adonis story, it is better to take women at face value than to seek their hidden truth: 'Se Reson vient, point n'an creez' [If Reason comes, don't believe her] (*RR*, 15730). The Lover puts this notion into practice with his ready belief that Bel Acueil remained impervious to la Vieille's instructions: 'ce me fiançoit et juroit, / autrement ne m'aseüroit' [he swore up and down, and gave me no other assurances] (*RR*, 12969–70). And despite all that he has been through with Faux Semblant and la Vieille, he will not believe that the Rose has ever been granted to anyone else, 'neïs se ce fust chose voire' [even if it was true] (*RR*, 21634). Knowledge of women seems to be included in the 'art of love' only so that it can be excluded from any actual love experience.

In this respect the Lover shows himself a ready pupil of Ami, who does not shrink from expounding feminine duplicity while nonetheless arguing that such matters are best forgotten. It is not the Jaloux's misogyny that Ami objects to, but his violent efforts to control his wife. Ami readily acknowledges that women are naturally unfaithful:

> N'est donc bien privee tel beste
> qui de foïr est tourjorz preste;
> tant est de diverse muance
> que nus n'i doit avoir fiance. (*RR*, 9883–86)

[Such a creature is not a good thing to be intimate with, being always ready to flee; it is so constantly changing that no one should trust it.]

But for that very reason, the best policy is to turn a blind eye: 'Ne ja riens contre li ne croie / por certeineté qu'il en oie' [Nor should he believe anything against her, whatever the certainty with which he hears about it] (*RR*, 9695–96). Ami's advice informs the narrator's comments on Adonis, as well as the Lover's faith in Bel Acueil. The overt insistence that women must always be believed masks a covert wink to the reader, acknowledging that of course they never can be; but we do it anyway. Suppressing knowledge of feminine wiles is a process integral to erotic desire.

But if this solution to the 'woman problem' seems acceptable in its Ovidian context, the question is reopened by Genius. In describing the fate of a husband who trusts his wife, Genius echoes Ami's words, while revealing their source in the *Aeneid*:

> Virgiles meïsmes tesmoigne,
> qui mout connut de leur besoigne,
> que ja fame n'iert tant estable
> qu'el ne soit diverse et muable.
> Et si rest trop ireuse beste. (*RR*, 16295–99)

[Virgil himself bears witness — he well knew their habits — that no woman has ever been so stable that she was not diverse and changeable. And she is a terribly irascible creature.]

Genius here cites Mercury's warning to Aeneas. Not the first message, in which Aeneas is told to leave Carthage; but the second, in which he learns that Dido is raising an army to thwart his plans: 'varium et mutabile semper / femina' (*Aeneid* IV, 569–70) [A fickle and changeful thing is woman ever].[7] And just as Mercury advises immediate flight, so too does Genius: 'Fuiez, fuiez, fuiez, fuiez, / fuiez, enfant, fuiez tel beste' [flee, flee, flee, flee, flee, boys, flee that creature] (*RR*, 16552–53). The explicit citation of Virgil sets Genius's tirade apart from the Ovidian teachings expounded elsewhere in the poem; it links him to the Jaloux, who also cites the *Aeneid*.[8] If, as we have seen, the Ovidian Orpheus exemplifies the dangers of doubting one's beloved, the Virgilian Orpheus illustrates the dire consequences of over-confidence and excessively ardent love. Considered from this Virgilian perspective, the gloss on Adonis suddenly sounds like a recipe for falling victim to a Dido — or to la Vieille.

As if identifying with Dido, whose story she tells sympathetically, la Vieille comments sadly on her own youthful generosity to the man she loved, who likewise abused and abandoned her. But she hopes to take her vengeance by training the next generation of girls to fight back: 'Ne m'en puis autrement vanchier / que par aprendre ma doctrine' [I cannot avenge myself any other way than by teaching my doctrine] (*RR*, 12848–49). The erotic femininity embodied by la Vieille or Dido offers itself freely, but exacts a terrible price in the end. One possible solution is to impose 'Lavinian' femininity onto the love object: she will be won in a heroic battle, a passive prize to be claimed by the victor. But if women are fundamentally mendacious and ever-changing creatures, how can a man be sure that this is what he has achieved? The short answer seems to be that he cannot. But this is why, as Ami argues, it is important to ensure that the true object of desire — sexual gratification — is never obscured by sentimental fancies. The allusions to Hercules's battle with Cacus that frame the conquest of the Rose suggest that the Lover has taken this sordid lesson to heart.

'Chascun cuide estre [...] Herculés'

Both allusions to Cacus closely follow the Virgilian text.[9] In his confrontation with
Poor, Seürtez summarizes Cacus's trick in dragging the stolen cattle backwards
so that no tracks would lead to his cave (*RR*, 15549–53; *Aeneid* VIII, 207–11). He
describes the monster's fear of the enraged Hercules (*RR*, 15543–48; *Aeneid* VIII,
220–24), and tells Poor, 'li meïstes es piez eles' [you placed wings on his feet] (15547),
paraphrasing Virgil's statement that 'pedibus timor addidit alas' [fear lends wings
to his feet] (v. 224).[10] The Lover later compares his assault of the Rose to that of
Hercules:

> .III. foiz a sa porte asailli,
> .III. foiz hurta, .III. foiz failli,
> .III. foiz s'asist en la valee,
> touz las, por ravoir s'alenee. (*RR*, 21593–96)

> [three times he assailed the gate, three times he struck it, three times he failed,
> three times he sat down in the valley, completely exhausted, to catch his
> breath.]

This too is a close paraphrase of Virgil's text: 'ter totum fervidus ira / lustrat Aventini
montem, ter saxea temptat / limina nequiquam, ter fessus valle resedit' (*Aeneid* VIII,
230–32) [Thrice, hot with rage, he traverses the whole Aventine Mount; thrice he
essays the stony portals in vain; thrice he sinks down wearied in the valley].

The sheer excess of the analogy casts the closing performance in an ironic light.
The decidedly unsentimental Lover feels himself gifted with superhuman prowess:
nothing, not even an intact hymen, can stop him. We see that he views the Rose
as rightfully his: it was stolen by Jalousie and hidden in the Tower, just as Cacus
hoarded the cattle that he stole from Hercules. According to Virgil, moreover,
Cacus was the son of Vulcan, an archetypical figure of male jealousy. Within the
Lover's ideological framework, then, the analogy might be justified. But the reader
is not obliged to share the Lover's perspective. For an opposing view, we need look
no further than the Jaloux, who comments contemptuously that the young men
courting his wife are 'si legiers et si volanz / que chascun cuide estre Rolanz, /
voire Herculés, voire Sanson' [such light-weights and so flighty that each one thinks
he is Roland, or indeed Hercules or Samson] (*RR*, 9151–53).

The violence of the passage — the idea that having sex with a maiden is like
killing a man-eating, fire-breathing monster — is part of Jean's salacious humour,
but it is also disturbing.[11] How, we might wonder, could this image possibly make
sense? One answer lies in the larger context of the citation: Aeneas hears the
story of Cacus from Evander, an ally in the war against Turnus. Hercules, freeing
Italy from a ravaging monster, is analogous to Aeneas, who will rid the land of
an unworthy would-be ruler even as he wins his bride.[12] Together with Genius's
warning against the feminine 'beste', the Virgilian citations cast the Lover as not
only Hercules, but Aeneas. Like Aeneas fleeing Dido, and unlike Orpheus turning
back to check on Eurydice, he will move confidently towards his goal. His sexual
prize will be won heroically, not received as a gift from a woman who will hold

him in her thrall. But if the tale of Hercules and Cacus reflects the grand narrative of sexual and imperial conquest, its presence in the *Rose* can only be ironic. Where Virgil implies an analogy of Hercules's battle with the war against Turnus, the Lover identifies the Herculean labour with the sex act itself. Medieval commentary tradition, moreover, glosses Hercules's victory over Cacus as representing the ability of wisdom and virtue to thwart vice by exposing it to the light of day: quite the opposite of what the Lover, with allies like Faux Semblant and Bien Celer, has in mind for the Rose.[13] And it need hardly be pointed out that the Lover is no Aeneas; his preoccupations are far from those of Virgil's pious hero. The Virgilian analogy exposes the Lover's grandiosity, while deflating Bel Acueil's optimistic assessment that 'il aime san guile' [he loves without guile] (*RR*, 21315).

Though Jean's immediate source is the *Aeneid*, Hercules's victory over Cacus is also mentioned in the *Consolation of Philosophy* (IV, m. 7).[14] After listing Hercules's accomplishments, Philosophy concludes:

> [...] pretiumque rursus
> Ultimi caelum meruit laboris.
> Ite nunc fortes ubi celsa magni
> Ducit exempli via! Cur inertes
> Terga nudatis? Superata tellus
>   Sidera donat. (IV, m. 7, 30–35)

> [and as his reward / For that last labour, heaven deserved. / Go then, you brave, where leads the lofty path / Of this great example. Why in indolence / Do you turn your backs in flight? Earth overcome / Grants you the stars.]

This meter occurs at the end of Book IV, and can be read in conjunction with the Orpheus meter, which closes Book III, and the first meter of Book IV, 'Sunt etenim pennae volucres mihi' [For I have wings swift flying]. All three focus on the ascent from worldly affairs to the Heavenly realm. Orpheus fails through his attachment to sensual desire; the two successful paths are philosophical study and noble deeds. The Lover rejected Reason's invitation to a contemplative life of ascetic study, with his sarcastic comment: 'Puis je voler avec les grues?' [Can I fly with the cranes?] (*RR*, 5393). The active life, however, is more appealing. And the notion that one can gain Heaven through labour of precisely the sort that the Lover most appreciates is expressed in the *Rose* by Genius, whose sermon opens with exactly that promise:

> et qui de bien amer se peine
> sanz nule pansee vileine,
> mes qui leaument i travaille,
> floriz en paradis s'an aille. (*RR*, 19505–08)

> [and whosoever exerts himself to love well, without any base thoughts, as long as he works at it loyally, may he go crowned in flowers to Heaven.]

A joint reading of the *Aeneid* and the *Consolation*, through the lens of Genius, underlies the Lover's self-congratulatory identification of his 'labours' with those of Hercules.

The closing allusion to Hercules and Cacus — the final Virgilian bracket framing the Lover's assault on the Rose — does, then, mark a resolution of sorts. Hercules slew the monster and recovered his cattle; Aeneas defeated Turnus and won Lavinia in marriage; the Lover routs Dangier and plucks the Rose. But any real sense of closure is possible only in a superficial reading. Even if the battle with Cacus is accepted as a mock-heroic analogy for the rambunctiousness of the youthful sex drive, there is a further problem with the Lover's chosen model: the fact that Hercules was destroyed by a woman.[15] As a model for heroic sexual conquest, Hercules is ambiguous at best. And like Aeneas with Dido, Hercules's demise illustrates the problem not of feminine resistance or infidelity, but of feminine desire. Deianira never intended to harm her wayward husband, but that has little bearing on her literary reputation. It is the Jaloux, once again, who reminds us of Hercules's fate:

> Cist Herculés ot mout d'encontres,
> il vainqui .XII. horribles montres;
> et quant ot vaincu le dozieme,
> onc ne pot chevir du trezieme,
> ce fu de Deïanira,
> s'amie [...] (RR, 9161–66)

> [This Hercules had many encounters, he vanquished twelve horrible monsters; and when he had conquered the twelfth, he could not overcome the thirteenth: that was Deianira, his beloved.]

Reason, echoing Alain's Natura, assures the Lover that it is entirely within his power to escape the force of erotic love: 'se tu le suiz, il te suivra, / se tu t'en fuiz, il s'en fuira' [if you follow it, it will follow you; if you flee, it will flee] (RR, 4327–28). It now seems, however, that the situation may not be quite so simple. As Genius's Virgilian warning implies, the venomous beast that is woman pursues with a vengeance any man who tries to escape her clutches; while Ami has already noted that she flees from any who attempt to possess her themselves. If this is true, then perhaps the best course of action is indeed to slay the monster; but by this time it is impossible even to say just what that monster is.

There is, moreover, a subtle reminder of the hapless Deianira in the Lover's Herculean labours. As Fleming has noted, Virgil's account of Cacus employs the term 'ter' [thrice] three times in as many lines; but the Lover's paraphrase adds a fourth '.III. foiz' to the series of actions, highlighting his grandiosity.[16] This supplemental set of three, I would argue, migrated into the Virgilian context from an Ovidian text describing, precisely, Hercules's battle with the river-god Achelous for the hand of Deianira. It is Achelous who narrates the struggle, during which 'ter sine profectu voluit nitentia contra / reicere Alcides a se mea pectora' (Met. IX, 50–51) [three times without success did Alcides strive to push away from him my opposing breast]. At different points Achelous fights in the shape of a serpent — 'longum formatus in anguem' [in the form of a long snake] (v. 63) — and a bull, but is bested in the end. The defeat of Achelous figures among the Herculean exploits listed in Boethius's poem (CP IV, m. 7, 23–24), strengthening its association both with the Cacus episode and with Hercules's translation into Heaven. It is appropriate that the Lover's super-hero image would incorporate not only a fight with a monster over stolen cattle, but also a battle for the possession of a woman — indeed, a 'pulcherrima virgo' (v. 9) [most beautiful maiden]. The intertextual configuration does, however, imply that the Lover is focused on overcoming obstacles that bar him from the Rose — Jalousie and her minions on the one hand, feminine fear and resistance on the other — without having considered the problems that might arise from the sexual liaison itself.

The analogy with Hercules, in other words, may seem to provide a reassuring answer to Genius's Virgilian warnings: the Lover has no fear of beasts or serpents, for he can overcome them all. But it also carries a sinister undertone, not only in its misogynistic disregard for female subjectivity, but also in its implications — equally misogynist — for the Lover himself. The deadly 'serpent' of which Genius warns is neither a male rival nor a jealous guardian, but the much-desired woman herself. Like so many young men enflamed by Cupid, the Lover fancies himself a heroic figure; but even the most triumphalist of models suggests that there is trouble — much trouble — ahead.

'Latet anguis in herba'

In his tirade following the exemplary tale of a man subjugated by his wife, Genius cites the famous warning from Virgil's Third *Eclogue*:

> et notez ces vers de Virgile,
> [...]
> anfanz qui cueilliez les floretes
> et les freses fresches et netes,
> ci gist li froiz sarpanz en l'erbe;
> fuiez, anfant, car il anherbe
> et anpoisone et anvenime
> tout home qui de lui s'aprime. (*RR*, 16556, 16559–64)

> [and note these lines of Virgil [...] you boys gathering flowers and fresh, clean strawberries, the cold serpent lies here in the grass; flee, boys, for it drugs and poisons and infects every man who comes near.]

So intent is Genius on stressing this point, in fact, that he immediately re-paraphrases the Virgilian verses at even greater length (*RR*, 16565–86). This passage opens a new 'bracket', that of the *Eclogues*, while also participating in the Virgilian intertextual space already opened by the *Aeneid* references. The bucolic imagery is appropriate to the Lover's goal of picking a flower; the warning might pertain to woman's corrupting allure, to her crushing disdain, or to her predatory designs. The sexual 'snake in the grass' has, in short, a myriad of possible interpretations, depending on whether it is seen in the context provided by Raison, Ami, Faux Semblant, la Vieille or Genius himself.

While Genius cites only two lines of *Eclogue* III, their larger context is illuminating. Virgil's poem presents a poetic contest between two shepherds, each of whom stakes a pair of carved wooden cups. One set bears the image of two astronomers:

> in medio duo signo, Conon et — quis fuit alter,
> descripsit radio totum qui gentibus orbem,
> tempora quae messor, quae curvus arator haberet? (*Ecl.* III, 40–42)

> [In the midst are two figures, Conon and — who was the other, who marked out with his rod the whole heavens for man, what seasons the reaper should claim, what the stooping ploughman?]

On the other set, the artist carved a wreath of acanthus, 'Orpheaque in medio posuit silvasque sequentis' (v. 46) [and in the centre placed Orpheus with the woods that follow him]. The cups of Virgil's sparring shepherd-poets emblematically present the opposition elaborated in Genius's sermon between natural cycles of fertility and harvest, with their attendant labours, and the seductive but sterile workings of Orpheus. Genius's citation of *Eclogue* III thus subtly prepares for the sermon to come. But if he recommends flight in this first intervention, the sermon offers a different model, in which the figure to be emulated is Cadmus. If sowing 'les denz d'un sarpent' [the teeth of a serpent] (*RR*, 19708) represents the act of procreation, what sort of 'serpent' did Cadmus kill: feminine resistance? sodomitic desire? the perverse pleasure taken in courtship indefinitely prolonged? Perhaps the serpent is simply the male member, which must be 'killed' and made to sow its 'teeth', or seed, in the female body. That Genius chooses to phrase his argument in Virgilian terms — citing the *Eclogues*, the *Georgics* and the *Aeneid* — is striking. Equally striking, however, is the extent to which this Virgilian wisdom is viewed through the lens of both Alain de Lille and Ovid. This is most apparent in Genius's sermon, to which I now turn.

'Labor omnia vicit'

Genius's image of procreation as ploughing is a *tour de force* of extended metaphor, whose most immediate source is the *De planctu*. Equally relevant, however, is Ovid's use of agricultural metaphors in the *Ars amatoria*, which parodies the *Georgics* in offering poetic instruction for erotic 'cultivation'.[17] In stressing the variety of seduction techniques needed to appeal to the kaleidoscopic range of feminine tastes and dispositions, for example, Ovid says:

> Finiturus eram, sed sunt diversa puellis
>   Pectora: mille animos excipe mille modis.
> Nec tellus eadem parit omnia; vitibus illa
>   Convenit, haec oleis; hac bene farra virent. (*Ars* I, 755–58)

> [I was about to end, but various are the hearts of women; use a thousand means to waylay as many hearts. The same earth bears not everything; this soil suits vines, that olives; in that, wheat thrives.]

This passage slyly echoes Virgil's admonition to study the soil before ploughing virgin ground, since not all crops thrive everywhere: 'hic segetes, illic veniunt felicius uvae, / arborei fetus alibi, atque iniussa virescunt / gramina' (*Georgics* I, 54–56) [Here corn, there grapes spring more luxuriantly; elsewhere young trees shoot up and grasses unbidden]. Virgil later gives a more extended discussion of soils, explaining which are best suited to the cultivation of olives, vines, grains, cattle and bees (II, 177–258). He identifies agricultural work as the epitome of virtue, contrasting the violence and greed of warriors with the simple life of the ploughman. Indeed, the rural life is humanity's closest approach to the Golden Age of Saturnian rule:

> hanc olim veteres vitam coluere Sabini,
> hanc Remus et frater [...]
> aureus hanc vitam in terris Saturnus agebat. (II, 532–33, 538)

[Such a life the old Sabines once lived, such Remus and his brother [...] such was the life golden Saturn lived on earth.]

But however innocent this praise of the rustic life may be, Ovid provided medieval readers with a classical model for the eroticization of Virgil's iconic imagery.

Genius adapts the Virgilian imagery still further in his exhortation to 'plough' the female body. Consider, for example, one of his extended pleas:

> Arez, por Dieu, baron, arez,
> et voz lignages reparez.
> [...]
> Secourciez vos bien par devant,
> ausinc con por cueillir le vant,
> ou, s'il vos plest, tuit nu saiez,
> mes trop froit ne trop chaut n'aiez.
> Levez au .II. mains toutes nues
> les manchereaus de voz charrues,
> formant au bras les soutenez,
> et du soc bouter vos penez
> raidement en la droite voie,
> [...]
> et les beus aus testes cornues
> acouplez au jous des charrues,
> resveilliez les aus aguillons.
>   (RR, 19671–72, 19675–83, 19691–93)

[Plough, for God's sake, barons, plough, and restore your lineage. [...] Hike up your clothing in front, as if to feel the breeze, or if you prefer, get completely naked, but don't get too hot or too cold. With your bare hands, lift up the frames of your ploughs, support them firmly with your arms, and strive to push the ploughshare stiffly in a straight path; [...] and harness your horned oxen to the yoke, liven them up with the goads.]

Genius's advice is an unacknowledged tissue of allusions to Book I of the *Georgics*:

> depresso incipiat iam tum mihi taurus aratro
> ingemere, et sulco attritus splendescere vomer. (vv. 45–46)

[then would I have my bull groan over the deep-driven plough, and the share glisten when rubbed by the furrow.]

> ergo age, terrae
> pingue solum primis extemplo a mensibus anni
> fortes invertant tauri. (vv. 63–65)

[Come then, and where the earth's soil is rich, let your stout oxen upturn it straightway, in the year's first months.]

> exercete, viri, tauros, serite hordea campis. (v. 210)

[my men, work your oxen, sow barley in your fields.]

> nudus ara, sere nudus. (v. 299)

[Plough naked, sow naked.][18]

Even the figure of the neglected or abused plough as a trope for sin finds its precedent in Virgil. Genius complains that 'les jaschieres, qui n'i refiche / le soc, redemourront an friche' [if the ploughshare isn't thrust into the furrows, they will lie fallow], and curses those who 'vont bestournant la charrue' [pervert the plough] (*RR*, 19543–44, 19618); Virgil, lamenting the perilous times, comments:

> quippe ubi fas versum atque nefas: tot bella per orbem,
> tam multae scelerum facies; non ullus aratro
> dignus honos, squalent abductis arva colonis
> et curvae rigidum falces conflantur in ensem. (*Geo.* I, 505–08)

[For here are right and wrong inverted; so many wars overrun the world, so many are the shapes of sin; the plough meets not its honour due; our lands, robbed of tillers, lie waste, and the crooked pruning-hooks are forged into stiff swords.]

As appropriated by Genius, Virgil's praise of the simple, virtuous life takes on a new and unexpected meaning.

Genius's one explicit citation of the *Georgics* occurs in his description of the decline of the Golden Age and the rise of agricultural and technological arts.[19] In Virgil's account, these arts were necessary for survival in a newly hostile environment: 'labor omnia vicit' (*Geo.* I, 145) [toil conquered the world], a sentiment echoed by Genius: 'toutes choses sunt vaincues / par travaill' [all things are conquered by work] (*RR*, 20146–47). Where Virgil focuses on activities vital to the provision of food and shelter, Genius argues for the procreative labour that literally enables the survival of the species. And if Virgil sees agricultural labour as the price that must be paid for the recovery of lost innocence and plenitude, Genius implies the same about sexual labours. The Heavenly Park to which Nature's followers are admitted surpasses anything hitherto known on earth, 'neïs quant regnoit Saturnus, / qui tenoit les dorez aages' [even those days when Saturn reigned, who held sway over the Golden Age] (*RR*, 20002–03). Genius's sexual reading of the *Georgics*, like his eroticization of the 'fleshly tablets' of II Corinthians 3, is possible because by this point the textual fabric of the *Rose* is utterly steeped in both the erotic doctrines of Ovid, and the procreative ideology of Alain de Lille.

'Omnia vincit amor'

If Genius argues that labour conquers all, Courtoisie cites a different Virgilian maxim: advising Bel Acueil to grant the Lover the Rose, she names the all-conquering force as love. Her source is explicitly identified:

> Biau filz, Amour vaint toutes choses,
> toutes sunt souz sa clef ancloses.
> Virgiles neïs le conferme
> par santance courtaise et ferme;
> quant *Bucoliques* cercheroiz,
> 'Amors vaint tout' i trouveroiz
> 'et nous la devons recevoir'. (*RR*, 21297–303)

[Fair son, Love conquers all things; all are under his lock and key. Virgil himself confirms it with a firm and courteous maxim; if you look in the *Eclogues*, you will find there 'Love conquers all, and we should accept it.']

In the Virgilian context, the overwhelming power of love has a sinister edge to it. The Tenth *Eclogue* portrays the dying Gallus, bereft of his lady, who has left him for another. Numerous figures attempt to bring Gallus to his senses. Arcadian shepherds ask him: 'unde amor iste' (*Ecl.* X, 21) [whence this love]? Apollo, no stranger himself to love, remonstrates with his poet: 'Galle, quid insanis?' (v. 22) [Gallus [...] what madness is this?] And Pan laments the brutality of love: 'Amor non talia curat; / nec lacrimis crudelis Amor nec gramina rivis / [...] saturantur' (vv. 28–30) [Love recks naught of this: neither is cruel love sated with tears, nor the grass with the rills]. But to no avail: proclaiming love irresistible, Gallus embraces death. *Eclogue* X offers a sketch, in miniature, that is analogous to the Lover's own persistence in pursuit of the Rose. Nor is this the first time that he has been associated with Gallus, who figures among the deceased love poets named by Cupid in the famous midpoint passage. The Lover proclaimed his own hopes of dying in Love's service on that same occasion:

> Atropos mourir ne me doigne
> fors en fesant vostre besoigne,
> ainz me praigne en meïsmes l'euvre
> don Venus plus volentiers euvre. (*RR*, 10341–44)

> [May Atropos not cause me to die unless it's in doing your work; may she take me in that very act that Venus most eagerly engages in.]

Whether or not he will literally die performing the 'work of Venus', we know that the Lover — 'Guillaume de Lorris' — will at least die in the process of writing a poem about that work. If not Venus's work, perhaps, then Cupid's.

This citation of the love-death of Gallus in the closing passage thus has the effect of relaying the reader from the poem's conclusion back to its midpoint — where, of course, the concluding lines of the poem have already been paraphrased (*RR*, 10569–72). Putting both passages together, we may conclude that Jean is both Ovid to Guillaume's Tibullus and Virgil to his Gallus. These are very different models, however, and — like so many elements of the *Rose* — not easily reconciled. Ovid portrays Tibullus as mourned by Venus and Cupid, and as beloved by both of his poetic ladies: 'cumque tuis sua iunxerunt Nemesisque priorque / oscula nec solos destituere rogos' (*Am.* III.ix, 53–54) [and Nemesis, and her thou lovedst before, added their kisses to those from thine own kin, and left not desolate thy pyre]. Virgil imagines Gallus as abandoned by his lady, his grief of no concern to the hard-hearted God of Love. The power of love, which Ovid sees as nurturing the poetic genius of Tibullus, is shown by Virgil to be a fatal passion that even poetry cannot overcome.

Again, from the Lover's perspective, the network of literary allusions ensures a satisfying closure to the erotic dream. He will not be waylaid by a Dido, or bitten by a snake, because he knows better than to trust a woman; but he will also avoid the desolation of Orpheus and the carnage of Adonis, because he can silence those suspicions when he needs to. Like Hercules, he overcomes all obstacles; he embraces the active path to Heaven, just as Genius advised. He has long since yielded to Love himself, and now Bel Acueil follows suit. Love — or at any rate, sexual desire — conquers even the most intractable resistance.

The Lover's insouciance, however, does not annul the moral reading implied by the Virgilian framework.[20] Conforming to the predictions of the Jaloux, the Lover shows himself to be an incautious and headstrong youth. If he perceives no serpent lurking around the Rose, this does not necessarily mean that none exists. The Lover shuns the temptations of pederasty, but he may still be following Orpheus, whose sensual love for Eurydice was the real cause of all his problems. And he certainly resembles Gallus: persistent in his mad fury, pursuing his desires unto death. From this moralizing perspective, the dreaded 'anguis in herba' might apply to those very poets with whom 'Guillaume de Lorris' is associated in the midpoint passage. The Virgilian couplet is in fact quoted in the *Policraticus* in a discussion of the merits and pitfalls of studying pagan philosophy (VII, 10). John of Salisbury calls for caution, noting that pagan writings contain both useful doctrines and dangerous errors. Employing a metaphor that works fortuitously to strengthen the relevance of this passage to the Lover's sexual campaign, he advises:

> Sic ergo legantur ut auctoritas non praeiudicet rationi; nam et urtica, dum rosa legitur, quandoque manum tangentis urit [...] quos si forte simplex lector ingreditur, semper poetici illius meminerit:
>> Qui legitis flores et humi nascentia fraga,
>> frigidus, o pueri, fugite hinc, latet anguis in herba.
> (ed. Webb, vol. II, p. 134)
>
> [Therefore let the pagan writers be read in a way that their authority be not prejudicial to reason; for the burning weed, as the rose is plucked, sometimes burns the hand of him who touches it [...] and should perchance any artless reader enter their field let him keep in mind this quotation: Flee hence, O ye who gather flowers / Or berries growing on the ground; the clammy / Snake is hiding in the grass. (tr. Pike, p. 255)]

For a reasonably well-informed reader, Genius's words recall not only Virgil himself, but also the *Policraticus* citation of those verses, sounding a warning most immediately applicable to the seductive pull of love poetry. First Guillaume and then, inevitably, Jean himself will join Gallus, Catullus, Tibullus and Ovid in the ranks of poets who died pursuing some phantom jouissance. For alas... love conquers all.

This, then, is the dilemma on which the poem ends. Does the omnipotence of love imply an inevitably tragic outcome to the Lover's chosen path? Is it a reminder of Original Sin, and of the irrational act whereby this sin is transmitted to each new generation at the moment of conception? Or have the words of Virgil once more been appropriated and subjected to an Ovidian reading? Bel Acueil acceding to Love, which conquers all, allows the Lover to realize his greatest desire; 'Guillaume de Lorris' will at least die happy. Moreover, the one consolation that Virgil does grant Gallus is that his love will be commemorated in poetry after his death: as the latter states, 'o mihi tum quam molliter ossa quiescant, / vestra meos olim si fistula dicat amores' (*Ecl.* X, 33–34) [O how softly then would my bones repose, if in other days your pipes should tell my love!]. This is precisely the gift granted to Guillaume by Jean — and indeed, albeit only in passing, to Gallus. Perhaps, then, poetry offers a solution after all: a consolation to grieving lovers, an inspiration to those in the grip of desire.

The competing tangle of discourses that threads through the *Rose* both reveals, and refuses to define, the amorous and sexual knowledge envisioned by Cupid when he 'commissions' the poem. The implicit dialogue of Ovidian and Virgilian positions, like the interplay of Ovid, Boethius and Alain de Lille, can be seen as an implicit and irresolvable disputation embedded in the fabric of the poem. Jean shows that neither a moralizing discourse nor the pleasures of erotic fantasy — *esperance, douz regart, douz parler,* even the shared male discourse of misogyny — are a lasting obstacle to sexual jouissance. Instead, they are the screen of seeming propriety in whose unspoken 'negative space' the drive to jouissance is realized. In a fallen world, after all, sexual desire is as inescapable as it is irrational.[21] As Genius says with regard to the conflict between holy virginity, and the need to be fruitful and multiply:

> Qui voudra respondre respoigne,
> je ne sai plus de la besoigne.
> Viegnent devin qui an devinent,
> qui de ce deviner ne finent. (*RR*, 19595–98)

[Let him who wishes to respond, do so; I know no more about this matter. Let theologians divine it, who never stop their divining.]

In the end, Jean leaves the reader to draw his or her own conclusions about both the love and the labour that conquer all.

Notes to Chapter 5

1. On the interplay of gender and knowledge, mind and body, in Jean's *Rose*, see Kay, 'Women's Body of Knowledge'.
2. On Virgil in the *Rose*, see Langlois, *Origines*, pp. 116–17.
3. These passages were well known to medieval readers. Aside from the battle with Cacus, for example, all are cited in Vincent of Beauvais's *Speculum Historiale*; see Jacques Berlioz, 'Virgile dans la littérature des *exempla*', in *Lectures médiévales de Virgile. Actes du colloque organisé par l'École française de Rome* (Rome: École française de Rome, 1985), pp. 65–120 (pp. 80–83, 108–09).
4. On the relevance to medieval literature of the Virgilian notion of subjecting passion to rational control, and Ovidian scepticism in that regard, see Fyler, '*Omnia Vincit Amor*', pp. 201–03.
5. For an example relevant to the *Rose*, see John of Salisbury's *Policraticus* VIII, 24.
6. As Faux Semblant boasts, he is embodied in both men and women (*RR*, 11159–84).
7. On this passage, see Fleming, 'Jean de Meun', pp. 90–91.
8. 'Car la lettre neïs tesmoigne / ou sisieme livre Virgile, / par l'auctorité de Sebile, / que nus qui vive chastement / ne peut venir a dampnement' [for indeed the written record bears witness, in the sixth book of Virgil, on the authority of the Sibyl, that no one who lives chastely can be damned] (*RR*, 8978–82; cf. *Aeneid* VI, 563).
9. See Fleming, 'Jean de Meun', pp. 94–97.
10. On this line and its influence on an illuminator of the *Rose*, see Heidrun Ost, 'Illuminating the *Roman de la Rose* in the Time of the Debate: The Manuscript of Valencia', in *Patrons, Authors, and Workshops: Books and Book Production in Paris around 1400*, ed. by Godfried Croenen and Peter Ainsworth (Louvain: Peeters, 2006), pp. 405–35.
11. See Desmond, *Ovid's Art*, pp. 75, 112–13.
12. Fleming, 'Jean de Meun', p. 95.
13. See Minnis, *Magister Amoris*, pp. 104–05.
14. On this meter see Lerer, *Boethius and Dialogue*, pp. 190–95.
15. This point is raised by Blumenfeld-Kosinski, *Reading Myth*, p. 77.
16. 'Jean de Meun', p. 95.
17. See Eleanor Winsor Leach, 'Georgic Imagery in the *Ars amatoria*', *Transactions and Proceedings of the American Philological Association*, 95 (1964), 142–54.

18. My translation; Fairclough has 'strip to plough, strip to sow'.
19. Genius does not use Virgil's name, but the citation is clear: 'Et, si con dit an *Georgiques* / cil qui nous escrit *Bucoliques*' [and, as he who wrote the *Eclogues* said in the *Georgics*] (*RR*, 20085–86). Lines 20089–150 are adapted from *Georgics* I, 125–46.
20. This reading is stressed by Fleming, who argues that Jean's Virgilian citations express a shared moral view of sexual passion as 'a dehumanizing insult to rational human nature that, in effect, reduces a human being to the level of the beasts' ('Jean de Meun', p. 92). The figure of Virgil stands in implicit opposition to the Ovidian eroticism of the *Rose* in a fourteenth-century reworking of the text that includes an interpolation comparing the mirror of Narcissus to that crafted by Virgil for the defence of Rome; see my *'Romance of the Rose'*, pp. 196–99 and, for the text of the interpolation, pp. 371–72.
21. On the importance of this point in the *Rose*, see Hill, 'Narcissus, Pygmalion'; Wetherbee, 'Literal'.

CONCLUSION

The Lover's Dream

credimus? an qui amant, ipsi sibi somnia fingunt?[1]

VIRGIL, *Eclogue* VIII, 108

In his intervention at the midpoint of the *Rose*, Cupid portrays the as-yet unborn Jean as a veritable saviour to lovers:

> si fleütera noz paroles
> par carrefors et par escoles
> [...]
> que ja mes cil qui les orront
> des douz mauz d'amer ne morront. (*RR*, 10611–12, 10615–16)

> [thus he will flute our words in the streets and schools [...] and those who hear them will not die from the sweet pains of love.]

From this we might anticipate a new *Remedia amoris* which, as Ovid claimed for his poem, will save lovers from suicide: 'Ne pereat, nostrae sentiat artis opem' (*Rem.*, 16) [lest he perish, let him learn the help my art can give]. The *Rose* does contain a *Remedia* of sorts — the discourse of Reason — which might console lovers by educating them out of their self-destructive passions; while the discourse of la Vieille might enable jilted lovers to benefit from Ovid's advice of considering their former mistress in the worst possible light. But such is certainly not Cupid's aim. Jean is to be the poet who makes manifest the Word of the God of Love; with his prayer to Lucina, Cupid even echoes Virgil's Fourth *Eclogue*, so that the 'prophecy' of Jean's birth parodies the Sibylline prophecy of Christ (*RR*, 10587–96; *Ecl.* IV, 8–10). Love's poet to the core — a parodic 'fool for God' — Jean 'sera si tres sages hon / qu'il n'avra cure de Reson' [will be such a wise man that he will care nothing for Reason]. And his poem will benefit its readers under one condition: 'que Reson n'i sait creüe' [as long as they don't believe what Reason says there] (*RR*, 10541–42, 10623). Like the misogynistic tirades, only more so, Reason's discourse is presented as something to be disbelieved. How, then, should we understand this concept of an irrational, though nonetheless didactic and consolatory, poem — and how does the *Rose* fulfil this promise?

One answer lies in Reason's argument with the Lover about textual glossing, discussed above in Chapter 4. Reason believes that poetry should use bodily, even sexual, imagery as a vehicle for philosophical truths; the Lover believes that it should use decorous language and metaphor as a euphemistic screen for erotic content. Reason's concept of glossing is illustrated in medieval exegetical and mythographic traditions, of which perhaps the most spectacular example in medieval French literature is the fourteenth-century *Ovide moralisé*.[2] The *Moralisé* poet notes that the fables of the *Metamorphoses* are not only lies but heresies, spelling damnation for anyone who takes them literally: 'Ensi fu fausse ydolatrie / Essaucie par poesie' [thus false idolatry was glorified by poetry] (*OM* V, 2752–53). In his gloss on the contest between the Pierides and the Muses, he turns the story on its head to identify the Muses with philosophical wisdom, while the Pierides are identified with the 'poeticas Musas' that misled Boethius's persona at the opening of the *Consolation*:

> Cestes seult apeler ribaudes
> Philozophie apertement,
> Se li bons Boëces ne ment. (*OM* V, 2703–05)

> [Philosophy was openly accustomed to calling them wanton, if the good Boethius does not lie.]

Banishing this pagan poetry outright, however, may seem a heavy price to pay for theological correctness. Misleading though the lies of poets may be, they also have an undeniable and indeed powerful appeal: 'lor science est vuide et vaine, / [...] / Combien qu'ele soit delitable' [their teaching is empty and vain [...] no matter how delightful it may be] (*OM* V, 2677–79). The *Moralisé* poet's alternative is the potent tool of allegoresis, whereby he transforms Ovid's poem of pagan deities, sexual passion and bodily mutations into one that is morally and doctrinally beyond reproach. Because it is not fiction but (supposedly) autobiographical fact, however, Ovid's love poetry has no allegorical potential. The *Moralisé* poet reads the *Amores* as a truthful, and disgraceful, chronicle of adulterous escapades, claiming that Ovid was exiled not only 'Por "l'Art d'Amour", qu'il ot escripte' [because of the 'Art of Love' that he had written], but also 'Quar Augustus l'avoit trouvé / Sor Corinne et dou fet prouvé' [because Augustus had caught him with Corinna and proven his guilt] (*OM*, XV, 7155, 7161–62). The light of reason enables the reader not only to distinguish poetic lies from truthful confessions, but also to judge which truths and which falsehoods are worthy of attention, and to draw the appropriate lessons in each case. In a reading that might have been elaborated by Reason herself, the *Moralisé* poet clarifies that the fables of the *Metamorphoses* are a dazzling integument for intellectually and spiritually edifying truths, while Ovid's embarrassingly graphic poems of love followed by exile reveal the just deserts of a wanton life.

The historical Jean de Meun was clearly well informed about allegorical and exegetical traditions, but this is not the project he pursues in the *Rose*. His persona, 'Johans Chopinel', will draw his inspiration not from Philosophy but from the personification of erotic desire, protectively wrapped in its very wings: 'je l'afubleré de mes eles', declares Cupid [I will cloak him with my wings] (*RR*, 10607). Unlike the wings of intellectual ascent that Philosophy offers Boethius (*CP* IV, m. 1), Cupid's wings serve less to strip away layers of illusion than to provide an alluring screen, from within which there emerges a discourse operating in direct opposition to Reason and her movement from body to spirit.

As I have shown, the *Rose* guides its readers through an extensive and intricate tour of Latin authors, both ancient and medieval. Since much of this 'tour' is implicit, and little or no contextual information is given even when citations are explicitly identified, one would have to say that the *Rose* presupposes, rather than provides, knowledge of these texts. But with the juxtapositions and layerings that the poem produces and the rereadings that it invites, Guillaume and especially Jean encourage their readers to discover new meanings in old texts. Even more to the point, the dynamic of this intertextual mosaic allows a different 'knowledge' to emerge: unspoken, but discernible nonetheless as a key to the poem's meandering pathways and sometimes puzzling disputations. It is this bodily knowledge of sexual pleasure, pain and desire that determines many of the textual reminiscences and associations throughout the *Rose*, and which therefore may be absorbed by a reader who engages with the poem.

To understand more fully this 'bodily' knowledge generated by the *Rose*, we must return to the poem's status as a dream, and to Guillaume's claims for its prophetic nature. During the five-year period between the dream and the composition of the poem, he implies, the poet-protagonist fell in love with a beautiful maiden whose favour he still hopes to attract. Jean, however, undermines this reading by allowing the Lover to pluck the Rose. Looking back to Guillaume's prologue from the vantage point of Jean's conclusion, we might assume that the dreamer, after waking up, not only met but successfully seduced the 'rose' maiden. But we could equally conclude that the dream comes true in that the dreamer experiences an orgasm both oneirically and in the flesh, at the point of waking. The 'truth' of the dream narrated by the poem is quite literally sexual, and in choosing this trajectory Jean could certainly be seen as eschewing the dictates of Reason. Concordant with the Lover's stated preferences, the poem will be the euphemistically worded, if thinly disguised, story of a nocturnal, or more properly matitudinal, emission. If we further take Cupid seriously — that an irrational reading of the poem will relieve the pains of desire — it is difficult to avoid the conclusion that the *Rose* is being offered as, in effect, a pornographic text, a cornucopia of sexual fantasies and erotic *doux parler* that culminates in sexual jouissance not only for the poetic persona, but also for the willing reader. Such an outcome does, of course, run counter to the advice of Genius. Perhaps Jean's authorial persona is an Orpheus after all.

That is not, of course, the only way that it can be read. The reader could be both entertained and instructed by the poem's elaborate, if unruly, set of teachings about the joys, fears, dangers, ruses and rewards of love, as well as the forms of desire excluded from Cupid's domain — prostitution, homoeroticism, incest. He might learn enough to embark on his own sexual conquests, or he might content himself with reflection on the wider ramifications of these central themes: desire and duplicity in politics and society, the power struggles that blight marriage, sexuality as part of natural cycles of fertility and procreation, love as a cosmic force. The poem could even be read by someone who actually did believe Reason, for whom the erotic dream would be the oneiric equivalent of Ovid's love poetry: an exemplary display of shameful indulgence and moral degeneration, whose didactic value lies in its shocking depiction of how not to behave. Indeed, in his correspondence with Christine de Pizan during the famous *querelle*, Pierre Col claimed that the *Rose* had served as a *Remedia amoris* for one of his acquaintances.[3] As I argued in Chapter 1, Jean offers several models for the *Rose*. It is Cupid's poem for the instruction and consolation of lovers, as well as a tale of passion and longing aimed at softening the feminine heart; and it is the Lover's fulfilment of his promise to Reason to return to literary and philosophical studies. I have argued that Jean overlays the opening scenes of the *Amores* and the *Consolation of Philosophy* in such a way that in his continuation, Reason plays a double role. She is Philosophy, recalling the scholar in thrall to the poetic Muses; and she is the Tragic Muse, attempting unsuccessfully — at least for the moment — to send the love poet back to more serious literary endeavours. It is for the reader to decide whether the resulting text is a tribute to Lady Reason or to the God of Love — or possibly to Genius and his procreative imperative. And readers have been debating this very point virtually ever since the poem was written.

In Chapter 2 I examined the myth of Narcissus as a parody of self-knowledge, and of learning as a process of remembering. Narcissus at the fountain represents the sterility of a self-knowledge that is limited to an unchanging, timeless contemplation of the body as an object of erotic desire. The Lover, gazing into the crystals of Narcissus's fountain, sees not only himself but also the entire allegorical Garden; this provides him with a context, at least, in which to situate his newly discovered sexual self-image. Cupid's arrows on the one hand, and his instructions on the other, interpellate the young dreamer and shape him into a lover at once courtly and Ovidian, while also fixing the idealized feminine qualities that will, henceforth, define his desire — and thus himself. It is with good reason that the complete, co-authored *Rose* is given the title *Miroër aus Amoreus*; it too is a mirror in which, through a *mise en abyme*, the male reader can behold himself as lover, imaginatively projecting himself into the allegorical dream and identifying with the progress, setbacks and ultimate success of the quest. The poem constructs its readers as desiring male subjects, shaping their desire for a feminine love-object. Ultimately, the poem grants them the experience — as if in a dream — of sexual gratification, if they but silence the voice of Reason. Granted, this process requires them to focus their sexual passions into the desire for a fictional image — one suspiciously mirroring their own sexual anatomy. But then, that is precisely what the Lover himself has done. Perhaps the poem is hinting that this is what all lovers do.

Avoiding the despair of Narcissus and the anxiety of Pygmalion, the poetic 'I' of the *Rose* never acknowledges, as either Lover or narrator, that the Rose is only a metaphor. He plumbs its depths — 'car je vouloie tout cerchier / jusques au fonz du boutonet' [for I wanted to explore all the way to the very depths of the bud] (vv. 21694–95) — but this does not mean that he explains the *senefiance* of this image. It is impossible to construct a single meaning for the Rose that is valid both in Guillaume's text — where the *bouton* is openly displayed in the Garden, available for smelling, kissing and visual contemplation — and in Jean's, where its meaning is far more narrowly sexual.[4] And although it is not difficult to see the closing lines of the poem as an allegory of sexual intercourse, they neither record not transmit to the reader any explicit knowledge of sex as a bodily experience. Anyone not already in possession of the anatomical 'facts of life' would be hard pressed to extract them from Jean's account. As the Lover comments in the poem's closing lines, 'de Reson ne me souvint' [I had no thought for Reason] (v. 21730): it is still glossing as euphemism, not glossing as explication, that interests him. Only by fully entering into the erotic fantasy of the text — by maintaining an irrational position to the end — can the reader achieve the state of bodily arousal necessary for a realization of sexual knowledge.

If the Rose remains unknowable throughout the poem, so too does the Lover himself. In the end, we might imagine the Lover as a Narcissus who never admits that the Rose is only a fictional manifestation of ideals within his own imagination; an Orpheus unconcerned with definitive possession or knowledge of the poetically constituted love object; an Adonis who wilfully believes the lies of women; a Pygmalion whose erotic art participates in a textual genealogy of poetic fictions, rather than a lineage of sexual deviancy.[5] But does this make him less deluded than his Ovidian counterparts, or more so? And are his divergences from these models authentic? Or are these imagined differences simply another trick of the endlessly deceiving mirror of love? Throughout the *Rose*, we look askance at the Lover, trying to understand him by analogy, glimpsing him in mythic and metaphorical figures, but never certain whether we are seeing what he is — or what he is not.

Overall, the *Rose* supports the conclusion that erotic desire is illusory. The object of desire meets an imagined need rather than a genuine one — which is fortunate, since it can never be possessed, or even known, in any real sense anyway. But the many facets of linguistic, artistic and symbolic artifice that go into the effort at accomplishing it keep the desire alive; and they also create the 'bubble' of fantasy whose 'outside' is bodily sex. In the *Rose*, masculine jouissance lurks at the inaccessible exterior of poetic fictions, of idealized images, of spiritual sublimation. It is subject to extensive and detailed legal, moral and social codes, yet always exceeds their regulatory efforts, eluding Reason's control, and remaining a law unto itself. It is that which is excluded from intimate bonding with a companion through a shared interest in erotic exploits: despite the Lover's intimacy with Ami, the latter is never present for any of the encounters with Bel Acueil, Dangier or the Rose. Completion of the erotic quest is the act that Narcissus failed to achieve, and that Orpheus and his followers fail to perform. It is the goal that cannot be named in the elaborately staged rituals of courtship and seduction. It lies outside all these but also depends on them to bring it into existence through their very refusal to name it.

The special language that is poetry works its magic by leaving something unspoken, by existing in counterpoint or opposition to some other, unstated discourse with which it is both mutually exclusive and mutually constitutive. Guillaume and Jean, in different ways, produce a discourse of sexual desire and fulfilment in part through the conspicuous exclusion of moral philosophy and chastity on the one hand, homoeroticism and incest on the other. The *Ovide moralisé* poet, for his part, produces a discourse of spiritual desire and fulfilment in part through the endlessly repeated suppression and banishment of erotic desire, pleasure and pain. Sexual knowledge, ultimately, is as impossible to communicate as knowledge of the divine; but poetry somehow grants access to both, even if only through a glass darkly.

Notes to the Conclusion

1. 'Can I trust my eyes? Or do lovers fashion their own dreams?'
2. For analysis of the techniques of narration and allegoresis employed by the *Moralisé* poet, see Blumenfeld-Kosinski, *Reading Myth*, pp. 90–136; Kay, *Place of Thought*, pp. 42–69. Virginie

Minet-Mahy analyses the use of allegory in the *Ovide moralisé* as well as other late medieval texts that can be seen as engaging in implicit dialogue with the *Rose*, in *Esthétique et pouvoir de l'œuvre allégorique à l'époque de Charles VI: Imaginaires et discours* (Paris: Champion, 2005). For a discussion of the *Ovide moralisé* as a 'correction' of the *Rose*, see my 'Rival Voices: Rewriting Ovid in the *Roman de la Rose* and the *Ovide moralisé*', in *Les Translations d'Ovide*, ed. by An Faems, Virginie Minet-Mahy and Colette Van Coolput-Storms (Louvain-la-Neuve: Institut d'Études Médiévales, forthcoming). I cite *L'Ovide Moralisé*, ed. by Cornelis de Boer, *Verhandelingen der Koninklijke Akademie van Wetenschapen te Amsterdam: Afdeeling Letterkunde*, vols 15, 21, 30, 36–37, 43 (1915–38).

3. 'En verité je cognois home fol amoureux, lequel pour soy oster de fole amour a emprunté de moy *Le Ronmant de la Rose*, et luy ay oÿ jurer par sa foy que c'est la chose qui plus li a aidié a s'en oster' [Truly, I know a man who was a foolish lover, who, in order to cure himself of foolish love borrowed the *Romance of the Rose* from me, and I've heard him swear on his faith that it was the thing that most helped him change his ways] ('Aprés ce que', in Hicks, ed., *Débat*, p. 106).

4. See Van Dyke, *Fiction of Truth*, pp. 77–78.

5. Allen describes Jean's ironic critique of sexual love as 'an Ovidian technique which, while revealing the illusions of love, permits it to stand as a textual creation', in *Art of Love*, p. 108.

WORKS CITED

Primary Sources

ALAIN DE LILLE, *De planctu naturae*, ed. by Nikolaus M. Häring, *Studi Medievali*, 19 (1978), 797–879

—— *The Plaint of Nature: Translation and Commentary*, by James J. Sheridan (Toronto: Pontifical Institute of Medieval Studies, 1980)

ATKINSON, J. KEITH, and ANNA MARIA BABBI, eds, *L'Orphée de Boèce au Moyen Âge: Traductions françaises et commentaires latins (XIIe–XIVe siècles)* (Verona: Fiorini, 2000)

AUGUSTINE, *Confessions*, ed. by P. Knöll and W. H. D. Rouse, trans. by William Watts, Loeb Classical Library, 2 vols (Cambridge MA and London: Harvard University Press, 2006)

Biblia Sacra iuxta Vulgatam Clementinam, ed. by Alberto Colunga, OP and Laurentio Turrado (Madrid: Biblioteca de Autores Cristianos, 1965)

BOETHIUS, *Consolation of Philosophy*, ed. by E. K. Rand, trans. by S. J. Tester, Loeb Classical Library (Cambridge, MA and London: Harvard University Press, 1973)

CICERO, *Laelius, on Friendship (Laelius De amicitia) and the Dream of Scipio (Somnium Scipionis)*, ed. and trans. by J. G. F. Powell (Warminster: Aris and Phillips, 1990)

GUILLAUME DE LORRIS and JEAN DE MEUN, *Le Roman de la Rose*, ed. by Ernest Langlois, Société des Anciens Textes Français, 5 vols (Paris: Champion, 1914–24)

—— *Le Roman de la Rose*, ed. by Félix Lecoy, Classiques Français du Moyen Âge, 3 vols (Paris: Champion, 1965–70)

HICKS, ERIC, ed., *Le Débat sur le Roman de la Rose*, Bibliothèque du XVe Siècle, 43 (Paris: Champion, 1977)

HUGH OF FOUILLOY, *The Medieval Book of Birds: Hugh of Fouilloy's 'Aviarium'*, ed. and trans. by Willene B. Clark (Binghamton, NY: Medieval and Renaissance Texts and Studies, 1992)

JOHN OF SALISBURY, *Frivolities of Courtiers and Footprints of Philosophers: Being a Translation of the First, Second, and Third Books and Selections from the Seventh and Eighth Books of the Policraticus of John of Salisbury*, by Joseph B. Pike (Minneapolis: University of Minnesota Press, 1938)

[——] IOANNIS SARESBERIENSIS, *Policratici, sive De nugis curialium et vestigiis philosophorum, Libri VIII*, ed. by Clemens C. I. Webb, 2 vols (Oxford: Clarendon Press, 1909)

Lai de Narcisus, in *Pyrame et Thisbé, Narcisse, Philomena: Trois Contes du XIIe siècle imités d'Ovide*, ed. and trans. by Emmanuèle Baumgartner (Paris: Gallimard, 2000)

[MACROBIUS] MACROBIO, *Commento al Sogno di Scipione*, ed. by Moreno Neri (Milan: Bompiani, 2007)

OVID, *Ars amatoria*, in *The Art of Love and Other Poems*, ed. and trans. by J. H. Mozley, Loeb Classical Library (Cambridge, MA: Harvard University Press; London: William Heinemann, 1969)

—— *Amores*, ed. and trans. by Grant Showerman and G. P. Goold, Loeb Classical Library (Cambridge, MA and London: Harvard University Press, 1977)

—— *Metamorphoses*, ed. and trans. by Frank Justus Miller, Loeb Classical Library, 2 vols (Cambridge, MA: Harvard University Press; London: William Heinemann, 1971)

—— *Remedia amoris*, in *The Art of Love and Other Poems*, ed. and trans. by J. H. Mozley, Loeb Classical Library (Cambridge, MA: Harvard University Press; London: William Heinemann, 1969)

Ovide moralisé, ed. by Cornelis de Boer, *Verhandelingen der Koninklijke Akademie van Weten-schapen te Amsterdam: Afdeeling Letterkunde*, vols 15, 21, 30, 36–37, 43 (1915–38)

VIRGIL, *Eclogues, Georgics, Aeneid*, ed. and trans. by H. Rushton Fairclough, Loeb Classical Library, 2 vols (Cambridge, MA: Harvard University Press; London: William Heinemann, 1969)

Electronic Source

'*Roman de la Rose* Digital Library' <http://romandelarose.org> [accessed 19 September 2009]

Secondary Sources

AKBARI, SUZANNE CONKLIN, *Seeing through the Veil: Optical Theory and Medieval Allegory* (Toronto: University of Toronto Press, 2004)

ALLEN, PETER L., *The Art of Love: Amatory Fiction from Ovid to the 'Romance of the Rose'* (Philadelphia: University of Pennsylvania Press, 1992)

—— 'Ars Amandi, Ars Legendi: Love Poetry and Literary Theory in Ovid, Andreas Capellanus, and Jean de Meun', *Exemplaria*, 1 (1989), 181–205

ANTONIETTI, PASCAL, '"C'est li mireors perilleus": Images et miroirs dans *Le Roman de la Rose*', in *Le Moyen Âge dans la modernité*, ed. by Jean R. Scheidegger, Sabine Girardet and Eric Hicks (Paris: Champion, 1996), pp. 33–47

ARDEN, HEATHER, *The Roman de la Rose: An Annotated Bibliography* (New York and London: Garland, 1993)

BADEL, PIERRE-YVES, *Le 'Roman de la Rose' au XIVe siècle : Étude de la réception de l'œuvre*, Publications Françaises et Romanes, 153 (Geneva: Droz, 1980)

BAUMGARTNER, EMMANUÈLE, 'L'Absente de tous bouquets', in *Études sur le 'Roman de la Rose' de Guillaume de Lorris*, ed. by Jean Dufournet (Paris: Champion, 1984), pp. 37–52

BERLIOZ, JACQUES, 'Virgile dans la littérature des *exempla*', in *Lectures médiévales de Virgile. Actes du colloque organisé par l'École française de Rome* (Rome: École française de Rome, 1985), pp. 65–120

BLUMENFELD-KOSINSKI, RENATE, 'Overt and Covert: Amorous and Interpretive Strategies in the *Roman de la Rose*', *Romania*, 111 (1990), 432–53

—— *Reading Myth: Classical Mythology and Its Interpretations in Medieval French Literature* (Stanford, CA: Stanford University Press, 1997)

BOUCHÉ, THÉRÈSE, 'L'Obscène et le sacré, ou l'utilisation paradoxale du rire dans le Roman de la Rose de Jean de Meun', in *Le Rire au moyen âge dans la littérature et dans les arts*, ed. by Thérèse Bouché and Hélène Charpentier (Bordeaux: Presses Universitaires de Bordeaux, 1990), pp. 83–95

—— 'Ovide et Jean de Meun', *Le Moyen Âge*, 83 (1977), 71–87

BRAET, HERMAN, 'Du portrait d'auteur dans le *Roman de la Rose*', in *Medieval Manuscripts in Transition: Tradition and Creative Recycling*, ed. by Geert H. M. Claassens and Werner Verbeke (Louvain: Louvain University Press, 2006), pp. 81–99

BROOK, LESLIE C., 'Learning, Experience and Narrative Stance in Guillaume de Lorris's *Rose*', *French Studies*, 49 (1995), 129–41

BROWNLEE, KEVIN, 'Jean de Meun and the Limits of Romance: Genius as Rewriter of Guillaume de Lorris', in *Romance: Generic Transformation from Chrétien de Troyes to Cervantes*, ed. by Kevin Brownlee and Marina Scordilis Brownlee (Hanover, NH: University Press of New England, 1985), pp. 114–34

—— 'Orpheus' Song Re-Sung: Jean de Meun's Reworking of *Metamorphoses*, X', *Romance Philology*, 36 (1982), 201–09

—— 'Pygmalion, Mimesis, and the Multiple Endings of the *Roman de la Rose*', *Yale French Studies*, 95 (1999), 193–211

—— 'Reflections in the *Miroër aus amoreus*: The Inscribed Reader in Jean de Meun's *Roman de la Rose*', in *Mimesis: From Mirror to Method, Augustine to Descartes*, ed. by John D. Lyons and Stephen G. Nichols, Jr (Hanover, NH: University Press of New England, 1982), pp. 60–70

BRUSEGAN, ROSANNA, 'L'Énumération et les chiffres du *Roman de la Rose* au *Tesoretto*', *Littérature*, 130 (June 2003), 48–67

BURGWINKLE, WILLIAM E., *Sodomy, Masculinity, and Law in Medieval Literature: France and England, 1050–1230* (Cambridge: Cambridge University Press, 2004)

CAHOON, LESLIE, 'A Program for Betrayal: Ovidian *Nequitia* in *Amores* 1.1, 2.1, and 3.1', *Helios*, n.s. 12 (1985), 29–39

CALABRESE, MICHAEL A., '"Make a Mark That Shows": Orphean Song, Orphean Sexuality, and the Exile of Chaucer's Pardoner', *Viator*, 24 (1993), 269–86

CERQUIGLINI-TOULET, JACQUELINE, 'Cadmus ou Carmenta: Réflexion sur le concept d'invention à la fin du Moyen Âge', in *What is Literature? France, 1100–1600*, ed. by François Cornilliat, Ullrich Langer and Douglas Kelly (Lexington, KY: French Forum, 1993), pp. 211–30

CHERNISS, MICHAEL D., 'Jean de Meun's Reson and Boethius', *Romance Notes*, 16 (1975), 678–85

CLAASEN, JO-MARIE, 'Literary Anamnesis: Boethius Remembers Ovid', *Helios*, 34 (2007), 1–35

CORBELLARI, ALAIN, *La Voix des clercs: Littérature et savoir universitaire autour des dits du XIIIe siècle*, Publications Romanes et Françaises, 236 (Geneva: Droz, 2005)

CRABBE, ANNA, 'Anamnesis and Mythology in the *De consolatione philosophiae*', in *Atti. Congresso internazionale di studi Boeziani, Pavia 5–8 ottobre 1980*, ed. by Lucia Obertello (Rome: Herder, 1981), pp. 311–25

—— 'Literary Design in the *De Consolatione Philosophiae*', in *Boethius: His Life, Thought and Influence*, ed. by Margaret Gibson (Oxford: Basil Blackwell, 1981), pp. 237–74

DESMOND, MARILYNN, *Ovid's Art and the Wife of Bath: The Ethics of Erotic Violence* (Ithaca, NY: Cornell University Press, 2006)

DORNBUSH, JEAN, '"Songes est senefiance": Macrobius and Guillaume de Lorris' *Roman de la Rose*', in *Translatio Studii: Essays by His Students in Honor of Karl D. Uitti for His Sixty-fifth Birthday*, ed. by Renate Blumenfeld-Kosinski, Kevin Brownlee, Mary B. Speer and Lori J. Walters (Amsterdam: Rodopi, 2000), pp. 105–16

DRAGONETTI, ROGER, 'Pygmalion ou les pièges de la fiction dans le *Roman de la Rose*', in *Orbis Mediaevalis: Mélanges de langue et de littérature médiévales offerts à Reto Raduolf Bezzola à l'occasion de son quatre-vingtième anniversaire*, ed. by Georges Guntert, Marc-René Jung, Kurt Ringger, Katharina Maier-Troxler and René Specht (Berne: Francke, 1978), pp. 89–111

EVANS, DYLAN, *Dictionary of Lacanian Psychoanalysis* (London: Routledge, 1996)

FLEMING, JOHN V., 'Jean de Meun and the Ancient Poets', in *Rethinking the 'Romance of the Rose': Text, Image, Reception*, ed. by Kevin Brownlee and Sylvia Huot (Philadelphia: University of Pennsylvania Press, 1992), pp. 81–100

—— *Reason and the Lover* (Princeton, NJ: Princeton University Press, 1984)

—— *The 'Roman de la Rose': A Study in Allegory and Iconography* (Princeton, NJ: Princeton University Press, 1969)

FREEMAN, MICHELLE A., 'Problems in Romance Composition: Ovid, Chrétien de Troyes, and the *Romance of the Rose*', *Romance Philology*, 30 (1976), 158–68

FRIEDMAN, JOHN BLOCK, *Orpheus in the Middle Ages* (Cambridge, MA: Harvard University Press, 1970)

FRIEDRICH, ELLEN L., 'When a Rose Is Not a Rose: Homoerotic Emblems in the *Roman de la Rose*', in *Gender Transgressions: Crossing the Normative Boundary in Old French Literature*, ed. by Karen J. Taylor (New York, NY: Garland, 1998), pp. 21–43

FYLER, JOHN M., '*Omnia Vincit Amor*: Incongruity and the Limitations of Structure in Ovid's Elegiac Poetry', *The Classical Journal*, 66 (1971), 196–203

GALINSKY, KARL, 'Ovid's Poetology in the *Metamorphoses*', in *Ovid: Werk und Wirkung. Festgabe für Michael von Albrecht zum 65. Geburtstag*, ed. by Werner Schubert, 2 vols (Frankfurt-am-Main: Peter Lang, 1999), i, 305–14

GALLY, MICHÈLE, *L'Intelligence de l'amour d'Ovide à Dante: Arts d'aimer et poésie au Moyen Âge* (Paris: CNRS Éditions, 2005)

GAUNT, SIMON, 'Bel Acueil and the Improper Allegory of the *Romance of the Rose*,' *New Medieval Literatures*, 2 (1998), 65–93

GIER, ALBERT, 'L'Amour, les monologues: Le *Lai de Narcisse*', in *Conjunctures: Medieval Studies in Honor of Douglas Kelly*, ed. by Keith Busby and Norris J. Lacy (Amsterdam and Atlanta, GA: Rodopi, 1994), pp. 129–37

GILBERT, JANE, '"I am not he": Narcissus and Ironic Performativity in Medieval French Literature', *Modern Language Review*, 100 (2005), 940–53

GOLDIN, FREDERICK, *The Mirror of Narcissus in the Courtly Love Lyric* (Ithaca, NY: Cornell University Press, 1967)

GREGORY, ROBERT, 'Reading as Narcissism: Le *Roman de la Rose*', *SubStance*, 12:2 [39] (1983), 37–48

GROSSE, MAX, *Das Buch im Roman: Studien zu Buchverweis und Autoritätszitat in altfranzösischen Texten* (Munich: Wilhelm Fink, 1994)

GUNN, ALAN M. F., *The Mirror of Love: A Reinterpretation of 'The Romance of the Rose'* (Lubbock, TX: Texas Tech Press, 1952)

GUYNN, NOAH, *Allegory and Sexual Ethics in the High Middle Ages* (New York: Palgrave Macmillan, 2007)

—— 'Le *Roman de la Rose*', in *The Cambridge Companion to Medieval French Literature*, ed. by Simon Gaunt and Sarah Kay (Cambridge: Cambridge University Press, 2008), pp. 48–62

HARDIE, PHILIP, *Ovid's Poetics of Illusion* (Cambridge: Cambridge University Press, 2002)

HARRISON, ANN TUKEY, 'Echo and Her Medieval Sisters', *The Centennial Review*, 26 (1982), 324–40

HELLER-ROAZEN, DANIEL, *Fortune's Faces: The 'Roman de la Rose' and the Poetics of Contingency* (Baltimore, MD: Johns Hopkins University Press, 2003)

HICKS, ERIC, 'Donner à voir: Guillaume de Lorris or the Impossible Romance', trans. by Deborah S. Reisinger and Christine Reno, *Yale French Studies*, 95 (1999), 65–80

—— 'La Mise en roman des formes allégoriques: Hypostase et récit chez Guillaume de Lorris', in *Études sur le 'Roman de la Rose' de Guillaume de Lorris*, ed. by Jean Dufournet (Paris: Champion, 1984), pp. 53–82

HILL, THOMAS D., 'Narcissus, Pygmalion, and the Castration of Saturn: Two Mythographical Themes in the *Roman de la Rose*', *Studies in Philology*, 71 (1974), 404–26

HILLMAN, LARRY H., 'Another Look into the Mirror Perilous: The Role of the Crystals in the *Roman de la Rose*', *Romania*, 101 (1980), 225–38

HULT, DAVID F., 'Closed Quotations: The Speaking Voice in the *Roman de la Rose*', *Yale French Studies*, 67 (1984), 248–69

—— 'Language and Dismemberment: Abelard, Origen, and the *Romance of the Rose*', in *Rethinking the 'Romance of the Rose': Text, Image, Reception*, ed. by Kevin Brownlee and Sylvia Huot (Philadelphia: University of Pennsylvania Press, 1992), pp. 101–30

—— 'Poetry and the Translation of Knowledge in Jean de Meun', in *Poetry, Knowledge and Community in Late Medieval France*, ed. by Rebecca Dixon and Finn E. Sinclair (Cambridge: D. S. Brewer, 2008), pp. 19–41

—— *Self-Fulfilling Prophecies: Readership and Authority in the First 'Roman de la Rose'* (Cambridge: Cambridge University Press, 1986)

HUOT, SYLVIA, 'Bodily Peril: Sexuality and the Subversion of Order in Jean de Meun's *Roman de la Rose*', *Modern Language Review*, 95 (2000), 41–61

—— 'Confronting Misogyny: Christine de Pizan and the *Roman de la Rose*', in *Translatio Studii: Essays by His Students in Honor of Karl D. Uitti for His Sixty-fifth Birthday*, ed. by Renate Blumenfeld-Kosinski, Kevin Brownlee, Mary B. Speer and Lori J. Walters (Amsterdam and Atlanta, GA: Rodopi, 2000), pp. 169–87

—— '"Finding-Aids" for the Study of Vernacular Poetry in the Fourteenth Century: The Example of the *Roman de la Rose*', in *Lesevorgänge. Prozesse des Erkennens in mittelalterlichen Texten, Bildern und Handschriften. Freiburger Colloquium 2007*, ed. by Eckart Conrad Lutz, Martina Backes and Stefan Matter, Medienwandel — Medienwechsel — Medienwissen, 11 (Zurich: Chronos, forthcoming 2010)

—— *From Song to Book: The Poetics of Writing in Old French Lyric and Lyrical Narrative Poetry* (Ithaca, NY: Cornell University Press, 1987)

—— 'Medieval Readers of the *Roman de la Rose*: The Evidence of Marginal Notations', *Romance Philology*, 43 (1990), 400–20

—— 'Polytextual Reading: The Meditative Reading of Real and Metaphorical Books', in *Orality and Literacy in the Middle Ages: Symbioses, Performances, Fictions*, ed. by Mark Chinca and Christopher Young, Utrecht Studies in Medieval Literacy (Turnhout: Brepols, 2005), pp. 203–22

—— *The 'Romance of the Rose' and Its Medieval Readers: Interpretation, Reception, Manuscript Transmission*, Cambridge Studies in Medieval Literature, 16 (Cambridge: Cambridge University Press, 1993)

—— 'Rival Voices: Rewriting Ovid in the *Roman de la Rose* and the *Ovide moralisé*', in *Les Translations d'Ovide*, ed. by An Faems, Virginie Minet-Mahy and Colette Van Coolput-Storms (Louvain-la-Neuve: Institut d'Études Médiévales, forthcoming)

—— 'Senshu University MSS 2 and 3 and the *Roman de la Rose* Manuscript Tradition', in *Medieval English Literature: Torches from the Ancient World*, ed. by A. V. C. Schmidt, David Wallace and Tomonori Matsushita (Bern: Peter Lang, forthcoming)

—— 'Women and "Woman" in Bodleian MS Douce 332: A Case of "Accidental Meaning"?', in *De la Rose: Texte, image, fortune*, ed. by Catherine Bel and Hermann Braet (Louvain and Paris: Peeters, 2006), pp. 41–58

—— 'The Writer's Mirror: Watriquet de Couvin and the Development of the Author-Centered Book', in *Across Boundaries: The Book in Culture and Commerce*, ed. by Bill Bell, Philip Bennett and Jonquil Bevan (Winchester: St Paul's Bibliographies; New Castle, DE: Oak Knoll Press, 2000), pp. 29–46

JAGER, ERIC, *The Book of the Heart* (Chicago: University of Chicago Press, 2000)

—— 'Reading the *Roman* Inside Out: The Dream of Croesus as a *Caveat Lector*', *Medium Aevum*, 57 (1988), 67–74

JAUSS, HANS-ROBERT. 'La Transformation de la forme allégorique entre 1180 et 1240: d'Alain de Lille à Guillaume de Lorris', in *L'Humanisme médiévale dans les littératures romanes du XIIe au XIVe siècle*, ed. by Anthime Fourrier (Paris: Klincksieck, 1964), pp. 107–44

KAMENETZ, GEORGETTE, 'La Promenade d'Amant comme experience mystique', in *Études sur le 'Roman de la Rose' de Guillaume de Lorris*, ed. by Jean Dufournet (Paris: Champion, 1984), pp. 83–104

KANDUTH, ERIKA, 'Der Rosenroman — ein Bildungsbuch?' *Zeitschrift für Romanische Philologie*, 86 (1970), 509–24

KAY, SARAH, 'Love in a Mirror: An Aspect of the Imagery of Bernart de Ventadorn', *Medium Aevum*, 52 (1983), 272–85

—— *The Place of Thought: The Complexity of One in Late Medieval French Didactic Poetry* (Stanford, CA: Stanford University Press, 2001)

—— *The 'Romance of the Rose'*, Critical Guides to French Texts (London: Grant and Cutler, 1995)

—— 'Sexual Knowledge: The Once and Future Texts of the *Romance of the Rose*', in *Textuality and Sexuality: Reading Theories and Practices*, ed. by Judith Still and Michael Worton (Manchester: Manchester University Press, 1993), pp. 69–86

—— 'Touching Singularity: Consolation, Philosophy, and Poetry in the French *dit*', in *The Erotics of Consolation: Desire and Distance in the Late Middle Ages*, ed. by Catherine E. Léglu and Stephen J. Milner (New York: Palgrave Macmillan, 2008), pp. 21–38

—— 'Women's Body of Knowledge: Epistemology and Misogyny in the *Romance of the Rose*', in *Framing Medieval Bodies*, ed. by Sarah Kay and Miri Rubin (Manchester: Manchester University Press, 1994), pp. 211–35

—— *Žižek: A Critical Introduction* (Cambridge: Polity, 2003)

KELLY, DOUGLAS, *Internal Difference and Meanings in the 'Roman de la Rose'* (Madison: University of Wisconsin Press, 1995)

KESSLER, JOAN, 'La Quête amoureuse et poétique: La Fontaine de Narcisse dans le *Roman de la Rose*', *Romanic Review*, 73 (1982), 133–46

KOTUŁA, KRZYSZTOF, 'Deux Méthodes de structuration du texte dans le *Roman de la Rose*: Le Cas des MSS Londres, British Library, Royal 19 B XII et Rouen, Bibliothèque Municipale 1056', *Scriptorium*, 61 (2007), 170–79

LANGLOIS, ERNEST, *Les Manuscrits du Roman de la Rose: Description et classement* (Lille: Tallandier ; Paris: Champion, 1910)

—— *Origines et sources du Roman de la Rose* (Paris: Thorin, 1890)

LEACH, ELEANOR WINSOR, 'Georgic Imagery in the *Ars amatoria*', *Transactions and Proceedings of the American Philological Association*, 95 (1964), 142–54

LERER, SETH, *Boethius and Dialogue: Literary Method in the 'Consolation of Philosophy'* (Princeton, NJ: Princeton University Press, 1985)

LEWIS, C. S., *The Allegory of Love: A Study in Medieval Tradition* (Oxford: Oxford University Press, 1936)

LUCKEN, CHRISTOPHE, 'Les Muses de Fortune: Boèce, le *Roman de la Rose* et Charles d'Orléans', in *La Fortune: Thèmes, représentations, discours*, ed. by Yasmina Foehr-Janssens and Emmanuelle Métry (Geneva: Droz, 2003), pp. 145–75

MAKOWSKI, JOHN F., 'Bisexual Orpheus: Pederasty and Parody in Ovid', *The Classical Journal*, 92 (1996), 25–38

MARTIN, EVA, 'Away from Self-Authorship: Multiplying the "Author" in Jean de Meun's *Roman de la Rose*', *Modern Philology*, 96 (1998), 1–15

MAZZOLI, GIANCARLO, 'Tragedia vs. Elegia: Genesi e rifrazioni d'una "scena" metapoetica ovidiana (Am. 3,1)', in *Ovid: Werk und Wirkung. Festgabe für Michael von Albrecht zum 65. Geburtstag*, ed. by Werner Schubert, 2 vols (Frankfurt-am-Main: Peter Lang, 1999), I, 137–55

McCAFFREY, PHILLIP, 'Guillaume de Lorris and Jean de Meun: Narcissus and Pygmalion', *Romanic Review*, 90 (1999), 435–49

McKINLEY, KATHRYN L., *Reading the Ovidian Heroine: Metamorphoses Commentaries, 1100–1618* (Leiden: Brill, 2001)

MINET-MAHY, VIRGINIE, *Esthétique et pouvoir de l'œuvre allégorique à l'époque de Charles VI: Imaginaires et discours* (Paris: Champion, 2005)

—— 'Le Songe: De la mort de l'auteur à la naissance du lecteur', in *Le Rêve médiéval*, ed. by Alain Corbellari and Jean-Yves Tilliette, Recherches et Rencontres, 25 (Geneva: Droz, 2007), pp. 193–220

MINNIS, ALASTAIR, *Magister Amoris: The 'Roman de la Rose' and Vernacular Hermeneutics* (Oxford: Oxford University Press, 2001)

MORAN, JO ANN HOEPPNER, 'Literature and the Medieval Historian', *Medieval Perspectives*, 10 (1995), 49–66

NICHOLS, STEPHEN G., 'Parler, penser, voir: *Le Roman de la Rose* et l'étrange: "Lucarne" du manuscrit au XIIIe siècle', *Littérature*, 130 (June 2003), 97–114

NOUVET, CLAIRE, 'An Allegorical Mirror: The Pool of Narcissus in Guillaume de Lorris' *Romance of the Rose*', *Romanic Review*, 91 (2000), 353–65

—— 'A Reversing Mirror: Guillaume de Lorris's *Romance of the Rose*', in *Translatio Studii: Essays by His Students in Honor of Karl D. Uitti for His Sixty-fifth Birthday*, ed. by Kevin Brownlee, Renate Blumenfeld-Kosinski, Mary B. Speer and Lori J. Walters (Amsterdam and Atlanta, GA: Rodopi, 2000), pp. 189–205

OST, HEIDRUN, 'Illuminating the *Roman de la Rose* in the Time of the Debate: The Manuscript of Valencia', in *Patrons, Authors, and Workshops: Books and Book Production in Paris around 1400*, ed. by Godfried Croenen and Peter Ainsworth (Louvain: Peeters, 2006), pp. 405–35

OTT, KARL AUGUST, 'Jean de Meun und Boethius: Über Aufbau und Quellen des Rosenromans', in *Philologische Studien: Gedenkschrift für Richard Kienast*, ed. by Ute Schwab and Elfriede Stutz (Heidelberg: Winter, 1978), pp. 193–227

PARÉ, GÉRARD, OP, *Le 'Roman de la Rose' et la scolastique courtoise* (Paris: Vrin; Ottawa: Institut d'Études Médiévales, 1941)

PAYEN, JEAN-CHARLES, 'L'Art d'aimer chez Guillaume de Lorris', in *Études sur le 'Roman de la Rose' de Guillaume de Lorris*, ed. by Jean Dufournet (Paris: Champion, 1984), pp. 105–44

PICKENS, RUPERT T., '*Somnium* and Interpretation in Guillaume de Lorris', *Symposium*, 29 (1974), 175–86.

POIRION, DANIEL, 'Les Mots et les choses selon Jean de Meun', *Information littéraire*, 26 (1974), 7–11

—— 'Narcisse et Pygmalion dans le *Roman de la Rose*', in *Essays in Honor of Louis Francis Solano*, ed. by Raymond J. Cormier and Urban T. Holmes (Chapel Hill: University of North Carolina Press, 1970), pp. 153–65

POMEL, FABIENNE, *Les Voies de l'au-delà et l'essor de l'allégorie au Moyen Âge* (Paris: Champion, 2001)

QUILLIGAN, MAUREEN, 'Words and Sex: The Language of Allegory in the *De planctu Naturae*, the *Roman de la Rose*, and Book III of *The Faerie Queen*', *Allegorica*, 1 (1977), 195–216

ROWE, DONALD W., 'Reson in Jean's *Roman de la Rose*: Modes of Characterization and Dimensions of Meaning', *Mediaevalia*, 10 (1988), 97–126

SCHIBANOFF, SUSAN, 'Sodomy's Mark: Alan of Lille, Jean de Meun, and the Medieval Theory of Authorship', in *Queering the Middle Ages*, ed. by Glenn Burger and Stephen F. Kruger (Minneapolis: University of Minnesota Press, 2001), pp. 28–56

SCHULTZ, JAMES A., 'Heterosexuality as a Threat to Medieval Studies', *Journal of the History of Sexuality*, 15 (2006), 14–29

SHARROCK, ALISON, 'Ovid and the Discourses of Love: The Amatory Works', in *The Cambridge Companion to Ovid*, ed. by Philip Hardie (Cambridge: Cambridge University Press, 2002), pp. 150–62

STAPLETON, MICHAEL, *Harmful Eloquence: Ovid's Amores from Antiquity to Shakespeare* (Ann Arbor: University of Michigan Press, 1996)

STEINLE, ERIC M., 'Versions of Authority in the *Roman de la Rose*: Remarks on the Use of Ovid's Metamorphoses by Guillaume de Lorris and Jean de Meun', *Mediaevalia*, 13 (1987), 189–206

STRUBEL, ARMAND, 'Écriture du songe et mise en œuvre de la "senefiance" dans le *Roman de la Rose* de Guillaume de Lorris', in *Études sur le 'Roman de la Rose' de Guillaume de Lorris*, ed. by Jean Dufournet (Paris: Champion, 1984), pp. 145–79

UITTI, KARL D., ' "Cele... [qui] doit estre Rose clamee" (Rose, vv. 40–44): Guillaume's Intentionality', in *Rethinking the 'Romance of the Rose': Text, Image, Reception*, ed. by Kevin Brownlee and Sylvia Huot (Philadelphia: University of Pennsylvania Press, 1992), pp. 39–64

—— 'From *Clerc* to *Poète*: The Relevance of the *Romance of the Rose* to Machaut's World', in *Machaut's World: Science and Art in the Fourteenth Century*, ed. by Madeleine Pelner Cosman and Bruce Chandler (= *Annals of the New York Academy of Sciences*, 314 (1978)), 209–16

VAN DER POEL, DIEUWKE E., 'Moderne en Middeleeuwse Lezers van de "Roman van de Roos" ', in *Wat is Wijsheid? Lekenethiek in de Middelnederlandse letterkunde*, ed. by J. Reynaert (Amsterdam: Prometheus, 1994), pp. 101–15

VAN DYKE, CAROLYNN, *The Fiction of Truth: Structures of Meaning in Narrative and Dramatic Allegory* (Ithaca, NY: Cornell University Press, 1985)

WALTERS, LORI, 'Author Portraits and Textual Demarcation in Manuscripts of the *Romance of the Rose*', in *Rethinking the 'Romance of the Rose': Text, Image, Reception*, ed. by Kevin Brownlee and Sylvia Huot (Philadelphia: University of Pennsylvania Press, 1992), pp. 359–73

WOOD, CHAUNCEY, 'La Vieille, Free Love, and Boethius in the *Roman de la Rose*', *Revue de Littérature Comparée*, 51 (1977), 336–42

WETHERBEE, WINTHROP, 'The Literal and the Allegorical: Jean de Meun and the "De Planctu Naturae" ', *Medieval Studies*, 33 (1971), 264–91

ZINK, MICHEL, 'The Allegorical Poem as Interior Memoir', trans. by Margaret Miner and Kevin Brownlee, *Yale French Studies*, 70 (1986), 100–26

—— 'Bel-Accueil le travesti du *Roman de la Rose* de Guillaume de Lorris et Jean de Meun à "Lucidor" de Hugo von Hofmannsthal', *Littérature*, 47 (October 1982), 31–40

INDEX